SOUTH HOLLAND PUBLIC LIBRARY

3 1350 00176 7815

P9-BYR-601

South Holland Public Library
South Holland, Illinois

GAYLORD

What Life Was Like

WHEN ROME RULED THE WORLD

The Roman Empire
100 BC – AD 200

What Life Was Like

WHEN ROME RULED THE WORLD

The Roman Empire
100 BC – AD 200

BY THE EDITORS OF TIME-LIFE BOOKS, ALEXANDRIA, VIRGINIA

SOUTH HOLLAND PUBLIC LIBRARY

CONTENTS

When Rome
Ruled the World

CENTURIES OF CONFLICT AND ACCOMPLISHMENT

According to legend, the ascent of Rome began with the fall of Troy. Escaping the destruction of that fabled stronghold by the ancient Greeks, the Trojan hero Aeneas sailed to Italy, where he wed the daughter of a king. Among his descendants were the twins Romulus and Remus, who were left to die as infants along the Tiber River, only to be saved and suckled by a she-wolf. When the twins grew up, they set out to found a city at the spot where the she-wolf rescued them, but they quarreled over which of them had first right to govern the place and give his name to it. Romulus stood atop the Palatine Hill and Remus atop the Aventine Hill, and each claimed divine sanction. Finally, the two came to blows, and Romulus prevailed, consecrating Rome with his brother's blood. As this tale foretold, aspiring rulers of Rome would compete no less fiercely among themselves than with their neighbors, sacrificing all in pursuit of power.

Before imposing their will on others, the Romans first had to throw off the Etruscans, masters of northern Italy, who took control of Rome in the late seventh century BC, not long after ancient settlements atop the Palatine and nearby hills coalesced into one community. Influenced by Greek culture, the Etruscans bequeathed to the Romans a writing system based on the Greek alphabet and the worship of Jupiter and other divinities closely related to the gods and goddesses of the Greek pantheon. However much they gained from their overlords, Romans longed to be free of them. Provoked by the rape of the Roman noblewoman Lucretia at the hands of an Etruscan prince, angry citizens led by the legendary Lucius Junius Brutus drove the last of the Etruscan monarchs into exile.

In the words of the Roman historian Livy, Rome was now a "free nation, governed by annually elected officers of state and subject not to the caprice of individual men, but to the overriding authority of law." Indeed, the Romans codified the laws of their young republic around 450 BC in the Twelve Tables. But those laws did not give all Romans an equal say. From the start the republic was dominated by a wealthy minority known as the patricians. The common citizens, or plebeians, agitated for

MONARCHY		REPUBLIC								
753 BC	ca. 615-510 BC	509 BC	ca. 490-443 BC	390 BC	ca. 343-290 BC	280-275 BC	264-241 BC	218-201 BC	149-146 BC	

Legendary founding of Rome by Romulus, a descendant of the mythical Trojan hero, Aeneas

Period of Etruscan monarchy; the last king, Lucius Tarquinius Superbus (Tarquin the Proud), overthrown by Romans led by Lucius Junius Brutus

The republic is established under two annually elected consuls, beginning with Brutus and Lucius Tarquinius Collatinus

Struggle for political position between patricians and plebeians

The Gauls capture Rome, but quickly withdraw

The Samnite wars; Rome gains dominance over central Italy

War with Pyrrhus and Greek cities in southern Italy; Rome controls most of Italy

First Punic War against Carthage; Sicily becomes a Roman province

Second Punic War; Romans repel Hannibal's invasion of Italy and conquer much of Spain

Third Punic War; Rome destroys Carthage and takes undisputed control of western Mediterranean; part of North Africa becomes a Roman province

greater influence and won concessions, but power remained largely in aristocratic hands.'

Although Romans continued to quarrel among themselves, they presented a strong front against foreign rivals. After Gauls swept down from the north and sacked their city in 390 BC, Romans seemed determined to be the aggressors rather than the victims. By 275 BC they had secured control of most of mainland Italy by subjugating the Samnites to the east and defeating the Greek king Pyrrhus and his allies among the Greek colonists to the south. Swelled by fresh recruits from those subject Italian peoples—who eventually gained citizenship—Roman legions and warships then went on to challenge the expansive North African kingdom of Carthage in the Punic Wars, which raged on and off for more than a hundred years. Finally, in 146 BC Rome claimed victory by razing Carthage (which later rose from the ashes as a Roman city).

The defeat of Carthage ushered in the turbulent era of the late republic. Romans were now masters of the western Mediter-

ranean and soon extended their empire, but success abroad heightened tensions at home. Plebeians burdened by debt and lengthy military service were losing their land to patricians who profited by the labor of slaves taken in battle. Some aristocrats sided with the common citizens—notably the brothers Tiberius and Gaius Gracchus, who proposed land reforms and other measures to benefit the poor. Such efforts provoked sharp opposition, however, and set the stage for civil wars that had less to do with political principles, in the long run, than with the rival ambitions of Roman commanders, who seemed driven to reenact the fabled feud between Romulus and Remus and fight to the death for supremacy.

In one such showdown, allies of Gaius Marius, who reformed the army and won plebeian support, lost out to Lucius Cornelius Sulla, a staunch conservative who ruled with an iron hand. That conflict was later eclipsed by an epic confrontation between two of Rome's mightiest generals—Pompey the Great, a backer of Sulla who helped put down the slave revolt led by the gladiator Spar-

LATE REPUBLIC

133-121 BC	107-100 BC	88-79 BC	73-71 BC	70 BC	60 BC	58-51 BC	49 BC	48-44 BC	44 BC

Gaius Marius elected consul seven times; reforms Roman army

Spartacus leads slave revolt

Caesar conducts series of campaigns to conquer all of Gaul; takes troops to Britain in 55 and 54 BC; Crassus is killed by Parthians in 53 BC

Caesar defeats Pompey at battle of Pharsalus; Pompey flees to Egypt and is killed upon arrival; sole rule of Julius Caesar

Tiberius and Gaius Gracchus propose populist land reforms; Rome conquers southern Gaul

Civil war between supporters of Marius and Lucius Cornelius Sulla; Sulla prevails and remains sole ruler for three years before abdicating

Consulate of Pompey the Great and Marcus Crassus

Formation of informal alliance, known as the First Triumvirate, of Pompey, Crassus, and Julius Caesar

Defying Senate orders to disband his army, Caesar crosses the Rubicon River and invades Italy, starting civil war

Caesar assassinated on March 15; his grandnephew, Octavian, designated as legal heir; civil war breaks out between Caesar's assassins and his successors

tacus and later achieved victories that added to the Roman Empire in the east; and Julius Caesar, a gifted patrician who made his mark politically by appealing to the plebeians and won renown militarily by conquering Gaul and invading Britain. Caesar first joined with Pompey and the wealthy Marcus Crassus to form the First Triumvirate, then later crossed the Rubicon River with his loyal troops in 49 BC and went on to crush Pompey and claim sole command of an empire that now encircled the Mediterranean.

Another power struggle ensued after foes of Caesar tried to revive the republic by assassinating him in 44 BC. Caesar's path to power was then retraced by his grandnephew and heir, Octavian, who formed the Second Triumvirate with the ambitious Mark Antony and Marcus Aemilius Lepidus before bidding for supreme power. After defeating Antony and his paramour, Queen Cleopatra of Egypt, Octavian assumed the title Augustus and ruled alone as Rome's first emperor. Even the Roman historian Tacitus, a strong critic of imperial rule, conceded that Augustus earned universal gratitude by granting Rome the "gift of peace."

With the reign of Augustus, Rome entered a long period of strength and stability. The greatness of the empire often had less to do with the emperors themselves, however, than with their resourceful aides and subjects. Roman rulers during this era varied in quality from men of high purpose like Augustus and Hadrian to dissolute figures like Caligula and Nero. But even the weakest emperors were propped up by deft administrators—who had begun their lives as slaves, in some cases, and rose by merit to high positions—and by commanders of privileged origins who took to the rigors of campaigning as if born to hardship. No less important to the welfare of the empire were the collective efforts of soldiers who guarded lonely frontiers, provincials who came to terms with their Roman masters and won citizenship, and women who guided the fortunes of their families as wives or widows, sometimes running businesses and dispensing patronage.

Despite the diligent efforts of rulers and their followers, the empire eventually weakened. After the collapse in AD 235 of the

EARLY EMPIRE

43-42 BC	36 BC	31 BC	27 BC-AD 37	AD 37-68	AD 69	AD 69-96	AD 79	AD 96-117	AD 117-138

43-42 BC: Octavian forms Second Triumvirate with Mark Antony and Marcus Aemilius Lepidus; Octavian and Antony defeat Caesar's assassins at battle of Philippi

36 BC: Lepidus is ousted from Triumvirate by Octavian

31 BC: Octavian defeats Antony and Cleopatra at Actium, giving Octavian mastery of entire Roman world; Egypt becomes a Roman province

27 BC-AD 37: Octavian assumes honorific title of Augustus, becoming Rome's first emperor; succeeded by his stepson, Tiberius, in AD 14

AD 37-68: Reigns of Caligula (37-41); Claudius (41-54); and Nero (54-68), last ruler of the Julio-Claudian dynasty

AD 69: After Nero's suicide, troubled Year of the Four Emperors: Galba, Otho, Vitellius, and Vespasian

AD 69-96: Flavian dynasty: Reigns of Vespasian (69-79), Titus (79-81), and Domitian (81-96)

AD 79: Eruption of Mount Vesuvius buries Pompeii and nearby Herculaneum

AD 96-117: Brief reign of Nerva (96-98) followed by reign of Trajan (98-117), under whom the Roman Empire reaches its greatest geographical extent

AD 117-138: Reign of Hadrian; orders construction of wall in northern Britain in AD 122

Severan dynasty—a ruling family of North African origins— Rome endured a half-century of instability before Diocletian restored order and appointed a coruler to govern the western half of the empire while he led the eastern half. In the fourth century AD, Constantine, the first emperor to embrace Christianity, reunited the empire under his sole authority and established Constantinople (at the site of Byzantium) as the new imperial capital. By the fifth century, the east and west were permanently divided, and the western empire fell prey to Visigoths, Vandals, and other invaders from the north, finally collapsing in AD 476 when a weak ruler named Romulus Augustulus was deposed by the Germanic chieftain Odoacer.

The legacy of Rome endured, however, and not only in the languages, laws, and monuments of lands that once formed part of the empire. We know the ancient Romans today through their eloquent words and images, and that testimony forms the foundation of this volume. Insights into the troubled lives of Roman rulers come to us from such perceptive writers of the early em-

pire as Plutarch, a Greek who saw the great Romans as inheritors of his proud culture and wrote sympathetically of their trials; Tacitus, a patrician who lamented the fall of the republic and dissected imperial corruption with words as sharp as lancets; and Suetonius, a court secretary under Trajan and Hadrian who drew on documents in the imperial archives (as well as common gossip) to probe the character of past emperors. Other Roman sources chronicle the experience of ordinary people—including court records, funerary inscriptions, letters, literature, and the vivid depictions of sculptors and muralists, some of whose works emerged with startling clarity from the volcanic debris of Mount Vesuvius, which buried Pompeii and nearby communities in AD 79.

These haunting glimpses of past glory bear witness to the lively preoccupation of the Romans with their society and their surroundings. More concerned with the here and now than with the hereafter, they took the world by storm and left it a different place—and in doing so, made sure that their deeds would never be forgotten.

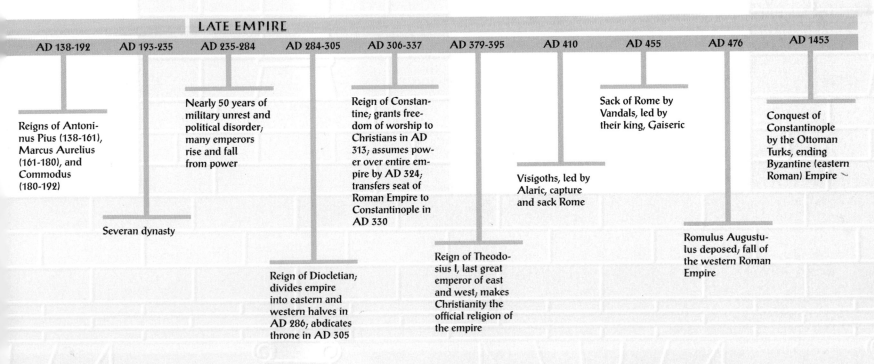

LATE EMPIRE

| AD 138-192 | AD 193-235 | AD 235-284 | AD 284-305 | AD 306-337 | AD 379-395 | AD 410 | AD 455 | AD 476 | AD 1453 |

Reigns of Antoninus Pius (138-161), Marcus Aurelius (161-180), and Commodus (180-192)

Severan dynasty

Nearly 50 years of military unrest and political disorder; many emperors rise and fall from power

Reign of Diocletian; divides empire into eastern and western halves in AD 286; abdicates throne in AD 305

Reign of Constantine; grants freedom of worship to Christians in AD 313; assumes power over entire empire by AD 324; transfers seat of Roman Empire to Constantinople in AD 330

Reign of Theodosius I, last great emperor of east and west; makes Christianity the official religion of the empire

Visigoths, led by Alaric, capture and sack Rome

Sack of Rome by Vandals, led by their king, Gaiseric

Romulus Augustulus deposed; fall of the western Roman Empire

Conquest of Constantinople by the Ottoman Turks, ending Byzantine (eastern Roman) Empire

BALTIC SEA

Hadrian's Wall
Vindolanda
York
Chester
BRITAIN

Bath
London
Dover

ENGLISH CHANNEL

Cologne
GERMANY
Rhine

GAUL

Danube

PANNONIA

DACIA

Nauportus

ALPS

BLAC

Nîmes

Rubicon
Tiber
ETRURIA
ITALY
Ostia
Rome
Arpinum
Naples
Herculaneum
Pompeii
Capri

APULIA

THRACE
Byzantium
(Constantinople)

BITHYNI

Philippi

MACEDONIA

ASIA MIN

SPAIN

SARDINIA

Pharsalus
Actium

Olympia
GREECE
Athens

SICILY

Carthage
Dougga

El Djem

AFRICA

MEDITERRANEAN SEA

Alexandria

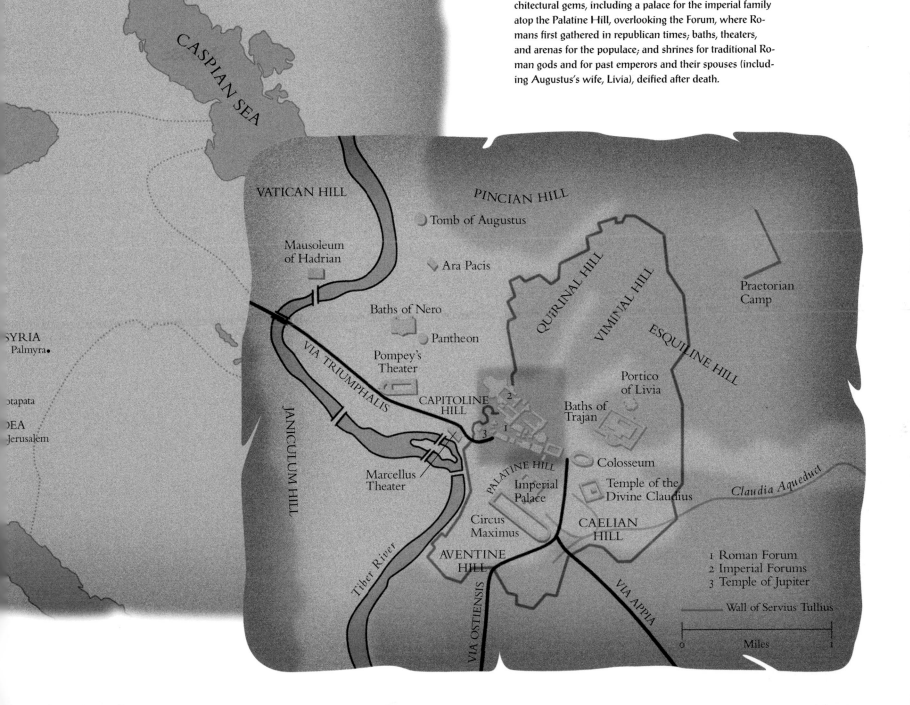

Graced with a genius for governing the lands they conquered, the Romans forged a prodigious empire, shown here in the early second century AD at its greatest extent *(within dotted border)*. From Britain to the banks of the Nile, people of sundry faiths rendered tribute to Caesar, as Augustus and his imperial successors were known.

The centerpiece of this empire was Rome itself *(below)*, situated alongside the Tiber River and resplendent with architectural gems, including a palace for the imperial family atop the Palatine Hill, overlooking the Forum, where Romans first gathered in republican times; baths, theaters, and arenas for the populace; and shrines for traditional Roman gods and for past emperors and their spouses (including Augustus's wife, Livia), deified after death.

CASPIAN SEA

SYRIA
Palmyra•

otapata

DEA
Jerusalem

VATICAN HILL

PINCIAN HILL

Tomb of Augustus

Mausoleum of Hadrian

Ara Pacis

QUIRINAL HILL

VIMINAL HILL

ESQUILINE HILL

Praetorian Camp

Baths of Nero

Pantheon

Pompey's Theater

Portico of Livia

Baths of Trajan

CAPITOLINE HILL

VIA TRIUMPHALIS

JANICULUM HILL

Marcellus Theater

PALATINE HILL

Imperial Palace

Colosseum

Temple of the Divine Claudius

Claudia Aqueduct

CAELIAN HILL

Circus Maximus

Tiber River

AVENTINE HILL

VIA OSTIENSIS

VIA APPIA

1 Roman Forum
2 Imperial Forums
3 Temple of Jupiter

—— Wall of Servius Tullius

0   Miles   1

CHAPTER ONE

THE STRUGGLE FOR POWER

Dressed in togas, senators and other Roman dignitaries join in a procession honoring Augustus. This scene is from the Ara Pacis, or Altar of Peace, commissioned in Rome in 13 BC to memorialize campaigns by Augustus that were credited with bringing peace to the empire. Like his granduncle and adoptive father, Julius Caesar, Augustus achieved supreme power, leaving Roman senators with little real authority.

aius Julius Caesar, recently proclaimed "perpetual dictator," entered the Roman Forum on the 15th day of February in 44 BC to preside over a rousing festival called the Lupercalia. No one could fail to recognize Caesar, seated as he was on a gilded chair on the elevated Rostra with a majestic purple robe around his shoulders. But he was not the sole object of attention. A great crowd had gathered to watch priests run through the Forum and around the Palatine Hill wearing hides and wielding strips of skin taken from goats sacrificed at the spot where Romulus and Remus, the fabled founders of Rome, were purportedly suckled by a she-wolf. Many of those lining the route were women who believed that the priests could grant them fertility by lashing them with the sacred goatskins.

Every Lupercalia was remarkable, but this year's festival went down in history because one of the participants did something startling and controversial. Among the priests who entered the Forum under Caesar's eye was Marcus Antonius, or Mark Antony, who had recently been chosen by Caesar to serve with him as co-consul. Traditionally, Rome's two consuls had been elected by the citizenry to lead the republic together for a term of one year, except in times of crisis, when one man was appointed to serve temporarily as dictator. By the time Caesar emerged as perpetual dictator, however, the consulship was his to do with as he pleased. He would hold the post for as many terms as he wished, and the man he put forward as his co-consul would do as he directed.

Mark Antony chose the occasion of the Lupercalia to pay Caesar a conspicuous tribute. Abandoning his run, Antony ascended the Rostra and offered the Roman ruler a crown. Caesar tactfully declined to put it on—a gesture that pleased many in the crowd, who did not care to see their leader take on the trappings of a king. Romans had ousted the Etruscan kings from their city centuries earlier and had equated royalty with tyranny ever since.

This was not the only time that someone in Rome tried to enhance Caesar's image with a crown. A wreath like the one Antony offered Caesar was reportedly placed around the brow of one or more statues of him in the city and duly removed by two tribunes, who were responsible for protecting the rights of the plebeians, or common citizens. Those tribunes were ousted from office as a result. According to the Greek biographer Plutarch, Caesar dismissed the two men because admirers had hailed their deed by likening it to the feat of the legendary Lucius Junius Brutus, who had driven the last Etruscan king from Rome.

There was more than one Brutus on Caesar's mind these days. He had reason to be concerned about the loyalty of Marcus Junius Brutus, who claimed descent from the old foe of tyrants and was well regarded by noble Romans who feared that Caesar was destroying their republican form of government. Now about the age of 40, or some 15 years younger than Caesar, Marcus Brutus had sided against him in his civil war against Gnaeus Pompeius Magnus, or Pompey the Great, but had since reconciled with Caesar and accepted from him a provincial governorship, among other honors.

The Forum, shown here in late imperial times, figured prominently in the life of Julius Caesar *(below),* who was offered a crown here by Mark Antony on February 15, 44 BC. A month later, Marcus Brutus spoke in the Forum in defense of Caesar's assassination, commemorated by a coin embossed with daggers and a cap of liberty *(far left).*

Caesar's regard for Brutus was as much personal as political. Many years earlier Caesar had entered into an adulterous affair with Brutus's mother, Servilia. The Roman historian Suetonius related that of all the women in Caesar's life, he loved Servilia best and lavished her with gifts, including a pearl worth an estimated 60,000 gold pieces. Some gossips went so far as to claim that Caesar was Brutus's natural father, although the affair with Servilia almost certainly began long after Brutus's birth.

People could only guess how the circumspect Brutus truly felt about Caesar. Did he esteem the man as his generous patron or resent him for carrying on with his mother? Restive Romans saw Brutus as a potential leader of the opposition to Caesar, Plutarch noted, and had been trying to goad him into conspiring against the dictator. "O that Brutus were alive!" one of Caesar's foes inscribed on a statue of Brutus's heroic ancestor. "You are asleep, Brutus," others wrote to him anonymously. "You are not a true Brutus." But who was the true Brutus, and where did his loyalties reside? The answer lay in his upbringing, and in long-nursed ambitions and grievances that led him to a fateful commitment.

Brutus's position as one of Rome's elite brought him both tremendous advantages and heavy responsibilities. The city's aristocrats lived in a manner far removed from that of the common citizens. Most Romans occupied small rooms over shops or rented cramped apartments in multistory tenements. Wealthy families, by contrast, had a large house in town and one or more estates in the country. Even their townhouses were typically gracious retreats from urban life, with an enclosed garden in back and an inviting atrium, partly open to the sky, in front, where the host as *patronus,* or patron, was visited regularly by his *clientes,* or clients,

Romans sought to protect children from evil spirits with a bulla, a circular charm like the one at right, made of gold. Boys wore them until the age of 14 *(left)*, girls until they married. Gold bullae were for the wealthy; those of poorer children were made of leather.

people of lesser stature who supported him politically in return for patronage. Close friends of the noble family were entertained in an intimate dining room, where they reclined on couches and were served by slaves, whose ranks included men and women of skill and refinement from Greece and other civilized places under Roman rule.

Despite such luxuries, aristocratic Romans did not necessarily lead soft or easy lives. Wealthy women amassed precious jewelry and kept up with the latest fashions in hairstyles, but they were fully prepared to leave the comforts of home and join their husbands on their tours as officers in the army or administrators in remote provinces. For leading families the purpose of acquiring a fortune was not to live idly but to succeed in public life—a costly proposition in Rome, where officials curried favor by sponsoring games and festivals and otherwise indulging the masses. And the reward for such expenditure was to achieve prominence in a public arena that had grown increasingly violent in recent times, as Rome grew mightier and the political stakes increased.

Marcus Brutus learned at an early age just how dangerous that arena could be. In 77 BC, when he was about eight years old, his father was executed by orders of his political foe, Pompey, during one of many civil conflicts that plagued the late re-

public. Servilia subsequently married Decimus Junius Silanus, who was later elected consul, but Brutus was raised by her half-brother, Cato the Younger. Cato led the conservative faction in the Senate called the optimates, who wanted to preserve old, unchanged republican traditions, including the privileges of the nobility, from whose ranks most senators, consuls, and other leading figures were drawn. The rival senatorial faction, known as the populares, were equally aristocratic but courted Rome's common citizens, who met in their own assembly and elected tribunes to look after their interests but still needed support from the powerful Senate, which controlled public finances, among other vital matters.

Julius Caesar was prominent among the populares and sparred frequently with Cato in the Senate. The sharp contrast between the two men extended to their dress. Cato, the arch-conservative, rejected the now-common custom of wearing a tunic under his toga, since the austere Romans of old did without that undergarment. Caesar, a man of some vanity who combed his thin hair forward to cover his balding pate, not only wore a tunic but added to it fringed wrist-length sleeves.

Caesar the *popularis* made himself all the more objectionable to Cato by sleeping with Servilia. On one occasion, it was said,

a note was passed to Caesar in the Senate. Cato ventured that it was probably treasonous, and Caesar passed him the note, which turned out to be a love letter from Servilia. "Keep it, you drunkard," Cato told Caesar, tossing the note back to him.

Servilia's affair with Caesar became common knowledge by the time Brutus was 20 and may well have been humiliating to him. But he was fortunate in having a passion of his own to distract him—an uncommon love of learning. Some wealthy young Romans cared more for exercising their bodies than their minds. Boys were often instructed in such combative arts as swordplay, horseback riding, boxing, and fencing. And noble families sometimes let their sons roam the streets with friends at night and get into mischief. "Come home from dinner as soon as possible," one

A mother watches her daughters play a game of chance by tossing so-called knucklebones resembling the ones below, carved from the anklebones of goats. Girls were supposed to confine themselves to such contests, while boys engaged in both this and rougher sport.

Roman writer advised, "for a gang of hotheaded youths from the best families is pillaging the city."

Brutus, however, was evidently the sort of boy who preferred studying to pillaging. Unless they enjoyed the services of a tutor at home, all boys of Brutus's class, and some girls, traipsed off at dawn to school accompanied by one or more slaves, who carried their tools of learning, including a stylus and wax tablet, and fended off seducers who preyed on children in the streets. The young pupils often met with their teacher in a public square or some other open place, where they wrestled with the perplexities of reading and arithmetic. Students who were too slow in untangling the texts when asked to recite, or too sloppy in copying lines of verse onto their wax tablets, might feel the teacher's cane. At midday, the pupils would be escorted home, to dine on bread, olives, cheese, dried figs, and nuts.

Brutus studied under a gifted teacher named Staberius Eros—a former slave who had been granted freedom—and made rapid strides. Even as he mastered the Latin texts, he took up Greek, a language considered essential for any Roman who wished to be truly cultivated. In his late teens, after he had cast off his boyhood robe for the manly *toga virilis*, he traveled to Athens to continue his education. There, centuries after the golden age of Athenian democracy, the city's philosophers still preached opposition to tyranny, a lesson that accorded with Brutus's family traditions. To be sure, democracy in Rome, like that in ancient Athens, was limited in scope. The vast population of Roman slaves had no rights at all, women could not vote or hold office, and noble families dominated the political scene. Yet Brutus cherished the liberties he and other Romans enjoyed to one degree or another under the republic.

Once he had completed his education, Brutus faced the challenge of achieving political honors in keeping with his distinguished ancestry and upbringing. One of the first tasks of a young Roman seeking success in public life was to marry well, which meant forging an alliance with another prominent household. Courtship in Rome could be a heartless business. Julius Caesar, for example, had been engaged in his teens to marry a girl whose family was rich but of the equestrian order, which put her one rung below his own senatorial order. Such matches served the interest of nobles intent on costly political careers, for the equestrians (so called because they originally served as cavalrymen in the army) tended to be wealthy landowners, bankers, and merchants. Before the planned marriage took place, however, Caesar broke the engagement to marry a young woman of the highest political pedigree, Cornelia, whose father served four terms as consul.

By the time Brutus was in his mid-twenties, Caesar's daughter, Julia—his only acknowledged child—was eligible for marriage, and Brutus may have been one of the candidates. The obstacles to the match were considerable, given Caesar's ongoing affair with Servilia and his feud with Cato, but marriage sometimes brought rival families together. As it turned out, the opportunistic Caesar found better political use for Julia by marrying her in 59 BC to Pompey the Great, a man some 30 years older than she, who joined with Caesar and Marcus Crassus, one of the richest men in Rome, to form the First Triumvirate. Together, the three men dominated the affairs of Rome for several years to come. The death of Julia in childbirth in 54 BC and Crassus's death a year later, however, severed the ties between Caesar and Pompey and helped set the stage for conflict between the two statesmen.

Brutus, meanwhile, had married the daughter of Appius Claudius, the head of one of Rome's oldest and proudest families. Social distinction did not prevent either Brutus or his father-in-law from seeking wealth and advancement in ways that may have been unseemly but were not uncommon

A slave arranges the hair of a wealthy young lady of Pompeii (near right).

BEAUTY AT ANY COST

For the wealthy Roman woman, the pursuit of beauty was a great challenge, filled with risks as well as rewards. The process began each morning when a slave girl brought her mistress bowls of scented water to wash off her night mask, normally a paste of flour and milk. Some masking creams were more exotic—the poet Ovid told of one for removing wrinkles that consisted of honey mixed with Libyan barley, narcissus bulbs, and crushed antlers from a healthy young stag. Still other creams were noxious, containing agents like mercury sublimate, which harmed the skin and could be poisonous.

After cleansing her face, brushing her teeth, and rinsing her mouth with a breath sweetener, the woman soaked in her scented bath (a luxury Romans of lesser means did without, resorting instead to public baths). Next she got a brisk rubdown from a servant called an unctor, or anointer, for the oils he applied. Then she put on her robe and passed into the hands of a maidservant called an ornatrix, or dresser, who saw to her mistress's hair, using combs and pins to achieve the preferred style, be it trailing braids or a bonnet of curls.

Few women were satisfied with their natural hair color. Some had it bleached

An ivory comb inscribed with the owner's name and carved bone hairpins helped to create coifs like the one seen here on Julia, wife of the emperor Domitian.

23

with a soapy compound imported from Germany, or darkened with a dye made of leeches and vinegar. Like the face creams, however, the dyes were sometimes too harsh, leading to hair loss and desperate efforts to promote fresh growth with deer bone marrow, bear's fat, and other remedies. When those measures failed, Roman women—like more than a few of their balding husbands—wore wigs.

The last task of the dresser was to apply her mistress's makeup from the vials that graced her dressing table, first lightening her complexion with white powder, then tinting her cheeks and lips with rouge derived from wine dregs or ocher, and darkening her eyelids with ash or kohl, an age-old Egyptian cosmetic. Finally, the lady dressed and donned her rings, bracelets, and brooches, crafted of precious stones from around the empire, and faced the world in high style.

A young woman pours perfume into a vial from a scent bottle like the one at lower right, made of gold-banded glass.

A Roman cosmetic chest holds a hand mirror and make-up applicators, among other beauty aids.

24

The funeral portrait of a woman in Roman-ruled Egypt shows off her fine jewelry, including a necklace resembling the one at right, made of gold, mother-of-pearl, and emeralds.

among ambitious Romans. Brutus, who accompanied his uncle Cato on official business to the island of Cyprus, lent money to the occupants of a city there at the extortionate interest rate of 48 percent. Appius Claudius, for his part, was brought to trial for misconduct as governor of Cilicia in Asia Minor and for offering bribes while campaigning for office. Brutus helped defend him and win his acquittal, but the incident must have been embarrassing for both men and given them cause to envy Caesar, who frustrated attempts by political opponents in Rome to prosecute him for his conduct in office by remaining abroad in Gaul as a provincial governor and general.

In 49 BC Caesar led his troops southward across the Rubicon onto Roman soil, thus challenging Pompey and the Senate and presenting Brutus with an agonizing choice. Should he side in the ensuing civil war with Pompey, who had executed his father, or with Caesar, who had slept with his mother and antagonized his uncle? Brutus cast his lot with Pompey, and was hailed by Cato and his fellow optimates as a man of honor for opposing the tyranny they attributed to Caesar. More of a scholar than a warrior, Brutus spent his spare hours in Pompey's camp reading and writing. Caesar retained a fond regard for Brutus out of love for Servilia and ordered his officers to capture him alive, Plutarch noted, or "if he made any resistance, to suffer him to escape rather than do him any violence."

As it turned out, Brutus survived the rout of Pompey's forces at Pharsalus in Greece in 48 BC. He slipped away unscathed and then wrote a letter begging pardon from Caesar, who in Plutarch's words not only "forgave him freely but honored and esteemed him among his chiefest friends." This calculated act of self-preservation contrasted with the path chosen by Cato, who ultimately fell on his sword rather than accept Caesar's pardon. Perhaps to atone for acting in a way the late Cato would have scorned, Brutus then divorced his wife and married Cato's daughter Porcia—a match Servilia disparaged. After all, Brutus gained nothing politically by marrying within the family.

Servilia, like many other forceful Roman matrons, took an unsentimental view of wedlock. She herself had evidently married for political reasons and sought romance elsewhere, although such conduct had its risks. The mere rumor of impropriety could have serious social consequences for women in particular. Caesar's second wife, Pompeia, for example, came under a cloud after a man entered her home disguised as a woman during a religious ceremony reserved for women. Caesar did not accuse her of adultery but divorced her anyway, explaining that he could not have her even suspected of wrongdoing.

Caesar himself, as a man and a powerful one at that, paid lightly for his domestic indiscretions. He might have to face some nasty quips, but it took something truly outlandish on his part to undermine his prestige. Caesar crossed that line when he took up with the Egyptian queen Cleopatra after pursuing the defeated Pompey to Egypt. Romans did not take kindly to the idea of their leaders consorting with foreigners. To make matters worse, Caesar then invited Cleopatra to Rome along with her young son Ptolemy XV, also known as Caesarion—a name that seemed to confirm widespread rumors that Caesar was his father. All of this fed fears that Caesar meant to set himself up as king, with Cleopatra as his queen, perhaps, and the foreign-born Caesarion as his heir.

Under the circumstances it might have seemed an obvious choice for Brutus to align himself with the Romans who were hostile to Caesar and who, by the time Mark Antony offered Caesar a crown at the Lupercalia in Febru-

A couple join hands at their wedding ceremony, a gesture also depicted on the ring above, given by a man to his fiancée at the time of betrothal. Weddings of wealthy Romans could be lavish affairs. The ceremony typically took place at the bride's home, followed by a sacrifice and wedding feast and concluding with a gala procession to the home of the bridegroom, where the bride was lifted across the threshold to prevent bad luck.

ary of 44 BC, were actively contemplating his assassination. After all, Brutus had signaled his devotion to Cato by marrying his daughter, and who could doubt that Cato, if he were still alive, would do anything that was necessary to end Caesar's dictatorship? Yet it was not just a matter of principle for Brutus. He was intensely ambitious, and he had to weigh his prospects under Caesar, who had already favored him with high office, against the opportunities that awaited him if Romans overthrew their ruler. According to Plutarch, Caesar sensed this keen longing in Brutus and wondered aloud how it would be satisfied: "I do not know what this young man wants, but everything that he wants, he wants very badly."

Caesar's patronage was now the only way upward, and it must have rankled Brutus, who had been a rising star in his own right, to find himself favored simply because Caesar wanted to please Servilia or placate his conservative foes. Mark Antony seemed comfortable playing the part of Caesar's grateful and admiring protégé, but it was hardly a congenial role for Brutus. In the end the only distinction that would satisfy him was the sort his uncle Cato and others of his family had achieved, under the rules of the republic.

It was not Brutus who initiated the conspiracy against Caesar, however, but his close friend and brother-in-law, Gaius Cassius Longinus. Cassius repeatedly urged Brutus, whose name was synonymous with opposition to tyranny, to lead the plot so that other men of stature would join. According to Plutarch, Cassius finally succeeded in enlisting Brutus in the assassination plot by asserting that supporters of Caesar would move to proclaim him king at a meeting of the Senate that would take place on the ides of March, or the 15th day of that month.

Caesar was not blind to the possibility that men close to him might defy him. Once, when told that Antony meant him ill, Caesar replied that it was not fat and luxurious men like Antony he feared but "pale, lean fellows" like Cassius and Brutus. Nonetheless, not long before his meeting with the Senate, Caesar dismissed his bodyguards, a group of loyal Spaniards. Perhaps he simply underestimated his foes. Or perhaps he was yielding to the deep fatalism that even the mightiest of Romans were subject to. Caesar often read the entrails of sacrificed animals or consulted augurs to see what the gods had in store for him, and recently the omens had not been favorable. A soothsayer named Spurinna, one of Rome's official augurs, told him that he was in grave danger, and that the threat would not pass before the ides of March.

As the day approached neither Caesar nor Brutus slept peacefully. A group of about 60 senators conspired with Cassius and Brutus to attack Caesar when he came before them on the 15th. Success depended on secrecy, and Brutus felt the strain of disguising his deadly intentions. "At home, and especially at night, he was not the same man," wrote Plutarch. Sometimes, his worries would invade his sleep and force him awake with a start. At other times, he was so preoccupied that Porcia could not help but notice that he was "full of unusual trouble."

To show Brutus that she was equal to his anguish and could be trusted with his secret, she gashed herself in the thigh with a small knife. When he rushed to comfort her, she reminded him forcefully that she was Cato's daughter, given to Brutus in marriage

"not like a concubine, to partake only in the common intercourse of bed and board, but to bear a part in all your good and all your evil fortunes." Moved by her fierce devotion, Brutus confided in Porcia by lifting his hands to heaven and begging the "assistance of the gods in his enterprise, that he might show himself a husband worthy of such a wife."

Caesar, for his part, was reportedly troubled by an ominous dream on the very eve of the ides of March. Like other Romans, he firmly believed that dreams could foretell the future. Once, in his younger days, after viewing a statue of Alexander the Great and bemoaning the fact that he had as yet done little to warrant comparison with that immortal conqueror, Caesar had dreamed of raping his mother, a vision that appalled him, Suetonius related, until soothsayers explained that it meant "he was destined to

conquer the earth, our universal mother." Now, on the night of March 14, he dreamed that he was "soaring above the clouds," Suetonius wrote, and "shaking hands with Jupiter," the greatest of gods. Such an encounter might be glorious, but to join the gods Caesar would first have to leave this world.

Caesar's third and last wife, Calpurnia, had feverish dreams of her own that night that were variously recounted in subsequent days. According to Suetonius, she dreamed that an ornament resembling the gable of a temple, placed atop Caesar's house by order of the Senate, came tumbling down, "and there he lay stabbed in her arms!" The next morning, she begged her husband to stay home, but he would not let it be said that he was slighting the Senate.

Caesar was carried through the streets in

"Yes, the ides of March have come, but they have not yet gone."

his litter to the appointed meeting place, Pompey's Theater, erected by his late foe and dominated by Pompey's statue. As he approached the building, he reportedly turned to the augur Spurinna and announced confidently, "The ides of March have come."

"Yes, they have come," Spurinna responded grimly, "but they have not yet gone."

When Caesar entered, the assembled senators—many of whom were ignorant of the plot—rose in his honor. The conspirators then gathered around him as he took his seat. A senator named Tillius Cimber pulled Caesar's robe down from his shoulder, a signal to the others that it was time to strike. Moments later, another conspirator, Servilius Casca, drew his dagger and struck Caesar a glancing blow to the throat. Then others pressed in, stabbing wildly. Several missed their target and wounded their fellow conspirators. Caesar at first resisted his attackers, Plutarch noted, but when he saw Brutus with his dagger drawn, he covered his face with his robe "and gave up his body to their blows." Some said Caesar died silently. Others claimed that when Brutus attacked, Caesar said to him in Greek: "You, too, my child?"

Caesar's assassins enjoyed only a fleeting triumph. They ran from Pompey's Theater out into the street, displaying their bloody hands and daggers to the startled onlookers and proclaiming the return of liberty. But they had given little thought to what they would do next, and they soon lost control of events. According to Plutarch, Brutus persuaded the other conspirators not to execute Mark Antony and instead tried to win Antony over, going so far as to allow him to read Caesar's will to the public at a funeral oration in the Forum. Caesar left to the people as a park his gardens beyond the Tiber River and willed a small sum of money to every Roman citizen. The bequest served to remind the crowd that Caesar had given thought to the common citizens. Antony further incited the crowd, Plutarch added, by displaying Caesar's bloody garment and pointing out "in how many places it was pierced."

ORGANIZING TIME

Among the devices Romans used to keep time were sundials like the one at lower left from Pompeii. Throughout the year, the period of daylight was divided into 12 hours, meaning that an hour in summer was longer than an hour in winter. Romans also consulted public calendars like the replica below, based on one in Rome, listing for each of the 12 months its name, zodiac sign, and protecting divinity; the number of days; the agricultural work to be done; and the festivals to be celebrated.

By Julius Caesar's era the discrepancy between the Roman calendar year and the solar year had caused the months to lag behind the seasons. To set things right Caesar extended the year 46 BC to 445 days and fixed the calendar year thereafter at 365 days, with an extra day in February every fourth year.

Fearing for their lives, the assassins fled the city. Other senators who supported them remained in Rome, but Antony seemed intent on claiming Caesar's mantle as supreme ruler. Caesar in his will had complicated Antony's plans, however, by adopting and naming as heir to the family fortune his 18-year-old grandnephew, Octavian (the future Augustus), who was abroad studying Greek literature. Despite his youth and a tendency to illness, Octavian had served energetically as Caesar's aide during a campaign against Pompey's hostile sons in Spain. Now all Rome would get a taste of the efficiency of this short, fair-haired, bright-eyed young man of regal bearing. Returning to Rome, he took charge of his granduncle's fortune and saw to it that Caesar's bequests were properly distributed.

Octavian and Antony were sharply at odds from the start. Octavian sided with Antony's foes in the Senate, led by the brilliant orator Cicero, who had not been informed of the assassination plot but heartily approved of the outcome. With backing from Cicero and his supporters, Octavian recruited troops and helped drive Antony and his depleted forces into exile north of the Alps, where they found refuge with the region's powerful governor, Marcus Aemilius Lepidus, a loyal aide to the late Caesar. Then, shifting sides with ruthless opportunism, Octavian abandoned Cicero and joined with Antony and Lepidus to form the Second Triumvirate. As part of the agreement, the three men drew up a list of 300 prominent enemies in Rome and had some of them executed. Among the victims was Cicero, whose head and right hand were severed by order of Antony and displayed in the Forum.

The triumvirs then turned their hostile attentions to the forces of Brutus and Cassius, who went down to defeat at Philippi in Greece in 42 BC. A short time before the battle, Plutarch related, the restless Brutus was visited in the night by a ghostly apparition who announced himself as Brutus's "evil genius" and warned ominously that Brutus would see him again at Philippi—to which Brutus responded calmly, "Then I shall see you."

RITES FOR THE NOBLE DEAD

Aristocratic Romans staged elaborate public funeral ceremonies to show *pietas,* or "respect," and to proclaim their distinction as a family. As shown above on a Roman sarcophagus, the body was carried through the streets from the home to the place of cremation atop a litter, reclining as if at a banquet.

Musicians led the grieving family, one of whom would deliver a eulogy from the Rostra when the funeral party paused in the Forum. Some wore masks of the deceased, and aristocrats honored the memory of their noble ancestors by keeping busts of them *(left).*

Perhaps the vision reflected a premonition on Brutus's part that his cause was lost and all that remained for him was to confront his demons and face the end bravely. After the defeat at Philippi, Brutus refused to flee for his life, insisting to friends that he was glad to die now and leave behind a virtuous reputation, while his conquerors would have to answer to posterity for usurping a "power to which they had no right." Then he followed the example of his uncle Cato and fell on his sword.

The victors ultimately divided up the empire, with Lepidus settling for control of northern Africa, while Antony took charge of the wealthy eastern provinces and Octavian presided from Rome over the western provinces. Before agreeing formally to those terms in 40 BC, however, Antony nearly clashed with Octavian, who had earlier agreed to marry Antony's stepdaughter Claudia but returned Claudia without consummating the union when he became embroiled in conflict with her strong-willed mother, Fulvia, and Antony's brother Lucius. Fulvia's death in 40 BC offered Octavian a chance to

Augustus's wife Livia *(left)*, portrayed as a traditional matron, exerted great influence over her husband *(right)*, shown as ruler of the world in a splendid breastplate detailing his triumphs.

repair relations with his fellow triumvir by wedding his sister, Octavia, to Antony.

That same year Octavian took as his own wife Scribonia, a relative of Sextus Pompeius, son of Pompey the Great. Sextus had been granted control of the Roman fleet by the Senate before the Second Triumvirate took power, and he had since bedeviled Octavian by blockading the coast of Italy and plundering merchant ships, preventing vital grain supplies from reaching Rome. Octavian and his in-law reached an uneasy truce in 39 BC, when Sextus agreed to raise the blockade while retaining control of Sicily and Sardinia.

By marrying for political purposes, Antony and Octavian had conformed to Roman aristocratic tradition. Both men were prey to passion, however, and became involved in heated affairs that altered their fortunes. In 39 BC Octavian fell in love with Livia Drusilla, a stately, attractive young woman of about 20. Livia had been married some five years earlier to Tiberius Claudius Nero, of the prestigious Claudian family. Livia's husband had sided with Antony's brother against Octavian, and they had been forced into exile with their infant son, Tiberius. Eventually they were permitted to return to Rome under an amnesty.

Octavian's romance with Livia was not the only affair attributed to him over the years. According to Suetonius, who admittedly passed along racy tales about Augustus and his imperial successors without vouching for their accuracy, Octavian consorted freely with the wives and daughters of his rivals, in part to discover what those men were up to. In one incident related by Antony and set down by Suetonius, Octavian hauled the wife of an ex-consul "from her husband's dining room into the bedroom—before his eyes, too!" Octavian brought the woman back some time later, blushing and disheveled. Livia had a special hold on Octavian, however. With her dignified bearing and fine aristocratic heritage, she appealed to him both personally and politically, and he was determined to have her as his wife. Whatever the feelings of her husband about the affair, he found it expedient to divorce Livia, who was pregnant at the time with their second child, Drusus.

Octavian was free to marry Livia because he had recently divorced Scribonia—a simple step in Roman society that could be initiated by either partner and was formalized when the couple separated and the woman got back her dowry. Octavian divorced Scribonia on the very day she gave birth to their only child, Julia, who remained thereafter with Octavian, as law and custom required, while Tiberius and his younger brother lived with their natural father until his death in 33 BC, when they joined Octavian. He and Livia would never have any children of their own.

Octavian's divorce severed his family ties to Sextus. To prevent the admiral turned pirate from again harrying Roman ships, Octavian called on the services of his close friend, the brilliant naval commander Marcus Agrippa, who crushed Sextus at sea in 36 BC. Octavian then pushed Lepidus into retirement, leaving the empire divided between two supremely ambitious men— Antony in the east and Octavian in the west.

Octavian's marriage to Livia, while hasty and unseemly, placed him securely within the privileged circle of Roman nobility that had long dominated affairs of state. Mark Antony was not so fortunate in his affections. His position as ruler of the eastern provinces had brought him close to Cleopatra, and like Julius Caesar before him, Antony succumbed to her charms, alienating Romans in the process.

The affair began in 41 BC, before the death of Antony's wife Fulvia and his subsequent marriage to Octavian's sister. Antony, then 42, summoned the 28-year-old Cleopatra to his quarters in Cilicia, where the admiring inhabitants had hailed him as Dionysus—or Bacchus, to the Romans—god of wine and bringer of joy. After delaying her departure from Egypt to show that she was not at anyone's command, Cleopatra arrived in grand fashion. As Plutarch pictured the scene, "She came sailing up the river Cydnus, in a barge with gilded stern and outspread sails of

33

SOUTH HOLLAND PUBLIC LIBRARY

purple, while oars of silver beat time to the music of flutes and fifes and harps." The queen lay under a canopy of gold cloth, he added, "dressed as Venus in a picture, and beautiful young boys, like painted Cupids, stood on each side to fan her. Her maids were dressed like sea nymphs and graces, some steering at the rudder, some working at the ropes. The perfumes diffused themselves from the vessel to the shore, which was covered with multitudes." Word raced through the crowd that "Venus was come to feast with Bacchus, for the common good of Asia."

As queen of a land that had achieved greatness long before Rome came into existence, Cleopatra considered herself equal, if not superior, to Antony, but she managed their meeting so skillfully

tra?" Antony added that he was now happily married to Cleopatra and wondered if Octavian was as devoted to his own wife: "Are you faithful to Livia Drusilla? My congratulations if, when this letter arrives, you have not been in bed with Tertullia, or Terentilla, or Rufilla, or Salvia Titisenia—or all of them. Does it really matter so much where, or with whom, you perform the sexual act?"

Unfortunately for Antony, Octavian's alleged affairs in Rome mattered far less to the public than Antony's flagrant relationship with a foreign queen. Some in Rome were afraid that the cunning Cleopatra wanted to shift control of the empire to Egypt, and Octavian helped to feed those fears by publicly de-

"She came sailing up the river Cydnus, in a barge with gilded stern and outspread sails of purple."

that he was charmed rather than offended. It was not so much her appearance as her force of character that held Antony spellbound. After following her back to Alexandria, he returned to Rome long enough to oblige Octavian by wedding his sister but ultimately went back to Egypt and his beloved Cleopatra.

In 32 BC Antony finally divorced Octavia in brusque fashion by dispatching orders to Rome that she leave his house there. By then, he already considered himself married to Cleopatra and had honored her by publicly declaring her son Caesarion to be the true child of Julius Caesar and assigning his own three children by Cleopatra territories in the east to rule. According to Suetonius, word reached Antony around this time that Octavian was incensed by the favors that were being shown Cleopatra, and Antony fired off an angry letter to his coruler in response: "What has come over you? Do you object to my sleeping with Cleopa-

nouncing Antony and his paramour as un-Roman. Octavian had long regarded himself as the rightful heir to Julius Caesar's political legacy as well as to his personal fortune. Now he set out to emulate Caesar by dispensing with his coruler and claiming supreme power for himself.

In the civil war that ensued, Antony and Cleopatra were outmaneuvered and lost their war fleet to Octavian and his admiral Agrippa at the Greek promontory of Actium in 31 BC. Antony and Cleopatra managed to escape by sea, but Octavian later descended on them in Egypt, where the two lovers took their own lives. Well aware that Antony had declared Caesarion the rightful son of Julius Caesar, Octavian had the youngster and potential rival tracked down and assassinated, thus bringing to an end the last of Egypt's dynasties. Henceforth, Octavian— or Augustus, as he became known in the year 27 BC, after

CLEOPATRA, QUEEN OF KINGS

Her actual beauty, it is said, was not in itself so remarkable that none could be compared with her," wrote Plutarch of Cleopatra *(left)*, but her charm "was something bewitching." She made men like Julius Caesar and Mark Antony, who were used to adulation, feel that she appreciated them uniquely. Plutarch noted that Plato wrote of only "four sorts of flattery, but she had a thousand."

But nothing Cleopatra said or did to honor her Roman admirers demeaned her own regal qualities. Part of the Ptolemy dynasty ruling Egypt since the death of Alexander the Great, she was Macedonian by ancestry and Greek by culture, but she considered herself an Egyptian, mastering the language and identifying herself with the goddess Isis. She hoped her relationships with Caesar and Antony would enhance her authority and shield Egypt from subjugation by Rome.

When Caesar arrived in Egypt in 48 BC in pursuit of his defeated foe, Pompey, the 21-year-old Cleopatra had been driven into exile by

A bust said to be of Cleopatra and a portrait of her on a coin—with Antony on the obverse—confirm that her appeal was not great physical beauty.

Ptolemy XIII, her 14-year-old half-brother, coruler, and husband (the Ptolemies practiced the old Egyptian royal custom of sibling marriage). Desperate for Caesar's support, she had herself wrapped in bedding, Plutarch related, and smuggled into the palace where Caesar was staying. Captivated by her wit and cunning, Caesar took her part against her brother, who died in defeat. As queen, Cleopatra then married her 12-year-old brother, Ptolemy XIV, but Caesar became her lover. Before he left Egypt, he cruised the Nile with her on her opulent pleasure barge.

Few Romans shared Caesar's fondness for her. Fears that she and her son Ptolemy

A Roman mosaic of life on the Nile portrays Egypt as a land of indulgence—an impression that Cleopatra encouraged when hosting Caesar and Antony, but that her Roman critics used against her.

XV—also known as Caesarion and believed to be Caesar's son—would claim power that belonged to Rome were not allayed even by Caesar's assassination, for she later took up with Mark Antony, who controlled the eastern half of the empire. Their passionate and notorious alliance was ultimately ended by Octavian, who invaded Egypt in 30 BC. According to Plutarch, she barricaded herself in the tomb prepared for her. Antony, thinking Cleopatra dead, fell on his sword, only to learn as he lay dying that she was still alive. He asked to be carried to her vault, where Cleopatra tore at herself in anguish, calling him "her lord, her husband, her emperor."

Soon after he died, she took her own life. By one account, she exposed herself to the bite of an asp, or cobra, an ancient symbol of pharaonic power. In the words of her handmaiden, she died in a manner befitting "the descendant of so many kings."

The deaths of Cleopatra and her son Caesarion, shown here as god-kings, marked the end of Egyptian independence.

returning triumphantly to Rome—would be lord of the Nile and undisputed master of the Roman world.

The astute Augustus had learned from the assassination of Julius Caesar not to flaunt the immense power he acquired. Augustus refused to be named dictator, while accepting the titles *princeps,* or "first citizen," and *pater patriae,* or "father of the country." He professed a desire to restore the republic, while establishing a virtual monarchy. He preserved the Senate and allowed its members to have their say, while taking upon the major duties they once exercised. As supreme commander, he was hailed as imperator, or conqueror, and from that imposing title came the term *emperor.* Certain Romans of the nobility may have despised him as they did his granduncle, but none dared make an attempt on his life, supported as he was by 4,500 Praetorian Guards and by the Roman masses, who were weary of civil strife.

At home as in public, Augustus tried not to appear too grand. He resided in a spacious, but not ostentatious, home on the Palatine Hill. He often refrained from the rich dishes that were served to his dinner guests and preferred to snack now and then on ordinary fare such as coarse bread, cheese, and green figs. He was also an "abstemious drinker," Suetonius noted, and limited himself at dinner in his later years to one pint of wine and water mixed: "If he ever exceeded this, he would deliberately vomit." In dress his major vanity was having the soles of his shoes thickened to make him seem taller—his height was listed as five feet seven inches, but that was an overstatement. His wife, Livia, also dressed simply. A sculptor portrayed her in a traditional ankle-length, pleated tunic known as a stola, draped with a soft, white palla, a blanketlike mantle. Augustus seldom let the various illnesses he was subject to interfere with his work, and in order to save time, he would have three bar-

increasing the rewards offered for those with large families.

Augustus also tried to rein in adultery. Under a law he enacted, a woman could divorce her husband for adultery but did not have to do so. Men, on the other hand, were required to divorce wives who had extramarital affairs and prosecute them for adultery. If convicted, a woman had to forfeit half her dowry.

Augustus wanted his only child, Julia, to be a model of feminine virtue. She spent her youth weaving and spinning, supervised at all times and permitted no boyfriends. As she matured, however, she may well have noticed the contrast between the chastity demanded of her and the lurid stories circulating about her elders, including her own father. (Suetonius passed along gos-

"Ah, never to have married, and childless to have died!"

bers cut his hair or shave him at one time, while he read or wrote.

Although he broke with tradition politically and was less than exemplary in his private affairs, Augustus was nostalgic about the old Roman ways and promoted time-honored religious practices and social standards. He restored more than 80 decaying temples and built a new one to Mars, the god of war, as part of a massive building program that provided work for laborers and overseers and buttressed the claim that he found Rome a city of bricks and left it a city of marble. As the guardian of public morality, he instituted laws to encourage marriage and reverse the declining birthrate. The provisions he imposed shortened the period allowed between betrothal and marriage; required widowers and widows to remarry; and penalized women who remained childless after the age of 20, men after 25. The penalties were unpopular, however, and Augustus responded by softening them and

sip that Augustus, even in his waning years, "still harbored a passion for deflowering girls—who were collected for him from every quarter, even by his wife!")

As an adult Julia rebelled against her strict upbringing and developed a reputation for promiscuity that escaped Augustus's attention for some time. After her first two husbands died, Julia was married to her stepbrother Tiberius, who was forced to divorce a woman he loved to wed Julia and came to resent her so deeply that he stopped sleeping with her. She sought consolation with other men in such flagrant fashion that Augustus finally took notice and resolved to punish her.

Although Julia was now a mature woman with children in their teens, her father had jurisdiction over her in his public role as Rome's moral guardian and in his private capacity as paterfamilias. Roman law gave the father of the house the power of life

HANDMAIDENS OF VESTA

No woman in Rome played a more important ceremonial role than the Chief Vestal, portrayed below in a sculpture from the House of the Vestal Virgins in the Forum. The priestesses who lived there were dedicated to Vesta, goddess of the hearth, and tended the eternal fire of Rome in the Temple of Vesta, depicted on the coin above.

The maidens were chosen between the ages of six and 10 and served for at least 30 years. It was said that if a vestal lost her virginity, the sacred fire would die out and Rome would suffer. Priestesses who failed to remain chaste were to be buried alive—a penalty imposed on the Chief Vestal Cornelia by the emperor Domitian.

and death over his children. Traditionally, a newborn was placed at the feet of the father, who would accept a boy by lifting him up and acknowledge a girl by ordering that she be fed. If, however, the newborn was deformed or otherwise undesirable, the father could have the child smothered, starved, or abandoned. Even as adults children remained subject to their father's sweeping authority. In theory he could sentence them to death if they offended him, although that harsh custom had all but expired by Augustus's time. More often, a father would disinherit an errant child.

The punishment Augustus meted out to Julia went beyond that. After denouncing her immoral behavior in detail to the Senate, he banished her to an island off the coast of Italy in 2 BC. She languished there for several years before being brought back to the mainland, where she remained in seclusion until she died in despair in AD 14, shortly after the death of Augustus himself. In his later years he had expressed his disgust with her by quoting wistfully a passage from the *Iliad:* "Ah, never to have married, and childless to have died!" Having cast off Julia, Augustus in fact died without a child of his own at hand. He was succeeded by Livia's son Tiberius.

Augustus's long reign had been one of internal peace and prosperity, and few Romans wanted to return to the old days, when rival aristocrats and their supporters battled ruinously for supremacy. But the rise of an imperial dynasty engendered its own problems. Struggles for succession that were once fought out between factions and families were now waged within the imperial household. And the candidate who prevailed was not always worthy of the honor.

Tiberius exemplified the problem of succession in that he was ill suited temperamentally for supreme power and won

In a wall painting from a dining hall in Pompeii,
a young slave relieves a guest of his sandals
(left), while another serves wine and a third
assists a diner who has overindulged *(right)*.

Roman appetites were piqued by scenes like the one at left, showing eggs and thrushes ready for cooking, and the cup below, decorated with skeletons and the motto Enjoy Life While Ye May.

PLEASURES BEYOND MEASURE

Writing in the first century AD, Roman satirist Petronius made light of the lavish banquets staged by newly wealthy men to impress their friends. "We took our places, and Alexandrian slaves poured water cooled with snow over our hands," remarked the narrator of Petronius's *Satyricon,* "while others approached our feet and with great skill began paring our corns." This gala was hosted by a man of newly acquired wealth named Trimalchio, who flaunted his many slaves and his rich cuisine, including dishes that made elegant fare like rose pie (recipe at right, from a Roman cookbook) seem plain by compari-

son. Among the treats he offered to his guests was a wine said to be 100 years old. "See how much longer-lived wine is than any poor mortal!" Trimalchio proclaimed. "Let's drink, then, and make merry, for wine is really life."

Few Romans were as extravagant as Trimalchio, but most would have agreed with him that there was no better way to seize the day than to share good food and drink with one's friends. The well-to-do gathered regularly in the evening for a banquet they called a *convivium* (living together), bringing men and often women and children together for feasting and

Rose Pie
Take roses fresh from the flower bed, strip off the leaves, remove the white [from the petals and] put them in the mortar; pour over some broth [and] rub fine. Add a glass of broth and strain the juice through the colander. [This done] take 4 [cooked calf's] brains, skin them and remove the nerves; crush 8 scruples of pepper moistened with the juice and rub [with the brains]; thereupon break 8 eggs, add 1 glass of wine, 1 glass of raisin wine and a little oil. Meanwhile grease a pan, place it on the hot ashes . . . in which pour the above described material; when the mixture is cooked, . . . sprinkle it with pulverized pepper and serve.

A floor mosaic from a Roman dining hall artfully mimics the bones, shells, rinds, and other debris that diners would toss aside for the help to sweep up.

A woman playing a cithara with her left hand and a harp with her right entertains diners at a banquet. Some lavish banquets featured after-dinner shows by mimes, acrobats, or dancing girls.

As portrayed in this wall painting, some male guests might linger after the banquet to enjoy the caresses of courtesans once the respectable women and children had retired.

mirth. Guest lists varied in size, but usually no more than nine people would convene in the host's *triclinium,* so called for the three couches arranged in a U shape around a table. Reclining comfortably, the guests were feted at length, then sent off with gifts or napkins filled with leftovers.

Banquets began with a *gustatio,* or appetizer, often consisting of eggs, shellfish, cheeses, dormice, and other tidbits, washed down with *mulsum,* a honeyed wine. Next came a main course of fish or meat, preferably wild game or a domestic animal that had been gorged on tasty items such as figs to enhance its flavor. Exotic entrées such as flamingo tongue were prized. More common items were dressed up. Thrushes, for example, might be arranged to resemble sea urchins floating in *garum,* a pungent sauce of fermented fish. Such strong seasonings helped to mask any hint of spoilage. Unlike mulsum, wine served with the meal was watered down. Most guests were full by the end of the main course, but no one wanted to miss dessert. If they couldn't find room for cake, custard, oysters, or snails, they might at least try some figs or apples.

Almost as appealing as the food was the setting, often decorated with splendid wall paintings and mosaics. Guests were expected to honor the host by arriving in good humor and good odor (having first visited the baths). Sometimes, perfumed doves were released to flutter about and scent the room. In between courses, slaves washed the diners' hands (Romans ate with their fingers). At Trimalchio's feast, slaves rinsed the guests' hands with wine, Petronius wrote, "for water was not good enough to wash in at that house."

Satirists were not the only ones to deride the excesses of the banquet table. "Where is the lake, the sea, the forest, the spot of land that is not ransacked to gratify our palates?" the Stoic philosopher Seneca lamented. "Our infirmities are the price of the pleasures to which we have abandoned ourselves beyond all measure and restraint." Yet thoughts of infirmity and death only encouraged indulgence. Few Romans wanted to live to be old and feeble, if that meant renouncing life's rewards. They could sympathize with the gourmand Apicius, who after squandering his fortune on pleasures of the palate, poisoned himself to death rather than eat like a beggar.

out because he had Livia's backing and because others Augustus might have preferred as his successor died prematurely. Tiberius had never been particularly close to his stepfather, who called him sour and stubborn. But Livia allegedly stopped at nothing to further Tiberius's cause—rumors sprouted up in Rome that she had caused the deaths of Augustus's preferred heirs, including his two grandsons by his disgraced daughter, Julia, and her ex-husband, Agrippa. Augustus did not suspect Livia of wrongdoing, however, and it may have simply been chance that thrust the moody Tiberius to the fore.

Once Tiberius became emperor, he chafed at Livia's still-pervasive influence. He needed her advice, Suetonius noted, but he did not want people "to think of him as giving it serious consideration." Tiberius saw no reason to thank Livia for what he felt was his due. Indeed, he had been a gifted general before becoming emperor, and he served capably for his first decade or so in power, maintaining order and prosperity. But he remained deeply insecure and grew increasingly remote from affairs of state, thanks in part to two men who exercised inordinate influence over him—his Greek astrologer Thrasyllus, and the prefect of his Praetorian Guard, Lucius Aelius Sejanus. While Tiberius was off at his villa on the island of Capri—where he spent the last decade of

A coin from Nero's reign reveals his close relationship with his mother, Agrippina the Younger. She later antagonized him and paid with her life.

Tiberius, an accomplished general before he succeeded Augustus as emperor, rides in triumph in a scene on a handsome silver cup.

his reign, heeding prophecies that danger awaited him in Rome—Sejanus tightened his own sinister grip on the capital by rounding up opponents on trumped-up charges of treason.

Sejanus evidently had imperial ambitions himself and plotted against members of the ruling family who stood in his way. He allegedly caused the death of Tiberius's son and heir apparent, Drusus, first seducing his wife and then arranging for him to be poisoned gradually, thus arousing no immediate suspicion. Sejanus later helped set Tiberius against two of of his grandnephews and would-be successors (one of whom died in exile and the other in prison) and might well have eliminated a third, Caligula, had not the emperor at last recognized Sejanus for what he was and had him executed. Rome thus escaped one menace only to fall prey to another—Caligula—who succeeded Tiberius upon his death in AD 37.

Caligula needed no Sejanus to brutalize Rome. He saw to the job himself, publicly humiliating senators, confiscating the wealth of citizens, and executing some who displeased him by forcing them into the arena, where they succumbed to wild beasts. His assassination in AD 41 brought to power his uncle Claudius, a retiring man of 50 with a limping gait and halting speech whose own mother regarded him as a fool—but who proved shrewd enough to survive Caligula's reign of terror and rule effectively for more than a decade. Yet the problem of succession came back to plague him. His last wife, Agrippina the Younger, Augustus's great-granddaughter, had been exiled for plotting against Caligula. In AD 54 she lived up to her devious reputation by poisoning Claudius with tainted mushrooms to ensure the succession of Nero, her son by a previous marriage. Like his predecessors, Claudius was deified after death, and Nero later quipped that mushrooms were the "food of the gods."

Only 16 years old at the time of his succession, the attractive young Nero at first ruled capably under the guidance of his tutor, the Stoic philosopher Seneca. His mother influenced him as well, but she seemed to bring out the worst in Nero. Early on, he appeared devoted to her in a way that some considered excessive. Mother and son often traveled together in her litter, reported Suetonius, and gossips claimed that behind the curtains he embraced her with "lecherous passion."

Whatever the nature of their bond, it eventually shattered. As the emperor grew more self-assured, Suetonius wrote, "the over-watchful, over-critical eye that Agrippina kept on whatever Nero said or did proved more than he could stand." First he deprived her of her honors, including her bodyguard, then he expelled her from the palace. When she continued to pester him, Nero decided to kill her. Three times, according to Suetonius, he tried to poison Agrippina, but she evidently knew what was coming and took an antidote. When he at last succeeded in doing away with her, in AD 59, he felt haunted by her spirit and hired Persian conjurers to summon her ghost and beg forgiveness.

Others close to Nero succumbed to his wrath. Blamed for the violent deaths of two of his wives and his stepbrother Britannicus, he later drove Seneca to suicide. Nero's notoriety was not confined to the imperial household. After a terrible fire ravaged large parts of Rome in AD 64, he at first provided relief for the victims but later built a lavish palace called the Golden House in a residential area cleared by the flames, fostering rumors that he had started the fire himself. Four years later, an armed insurrection by provincial governors impelled him to take his own life, and the dynasty initiated so promisingly by Augustus came to a pitiful end.

After a year of civil strife that saw power change hands four times, the general Vespasian installed himself as emperor and inaugurated a short-lived dynasty that ended with the assassination of his younger son, Domitian, in AD 96. Domitian's successor, Nerva, was childless and found a novel solution to the problem of succession by looking for a protégé outside his family—and homeland. He adopted as his son and next-in-line a Spanish-born

Standing in the Forum, the emperor Hadrian eulogizes his wife, Sabina, who died around AD 136. Although Hadrian deified his wife after her death, their relationship was far from idyllic. He once said that had he not been emperor, he would have divorced Sabina for her disagreeable character.

commander and governor of proven merit, Trajan. Under the energetic Trajan, the empire expanded to its greatest extent. At his death in AD 117, he was succeeded by his ward and relative, Hadrian, another man of Spanish heritage who honed his skills as a commander and governor before assuming power.

Hadrian styled his reign a golden age, and indeed his 21-year rule was a time of stability and prosperity. In some respects he resembled Augustus, launching an ambitious building program, not only in Rome but also in many provincial cities, and laboring to improve the army and the administration of the empire. In other ways, however, Hadrian broke the imperial mold. Many of his predecessors had prided themselves on conquest, but Hadrian sought no new territories, and he actually withdrew from lands that had been claimed by Trajan, concentrating instead on consolidating the empire and on rendering it more secure. Overall, Hadrian was less concerned with Rome and its pretensions than with the provinces. He spent most of his time touring the empire, taking advantage of the remarkable Roman network of stone-paved highways, built largely for military purposes. He made his way on foot or on horseback, bareheaded in the sun or snow, refusing to avail himself of the horse-drawn chariots or wagons favored by other travelers who could afford them.

In his later years Hadrian spent much of his time in the east. He was the first emperor to sport a beard, perhaps in tribute to the Greek philosophers he had come to admire so much. He also entered into a close relationship with a handsome young man by the name of Antinous, from the Greek-speaking region of Bithynia in Asia Minor. (Hadrian's marriage to Sabina, Trajan's grandniece, was strained and yielded no children.) But while visiting Egypt in Hadrian's company in AD 130, Antinous drowned, around the age of 20. Some claimed he jumped into the river Nile after being told he could prolong Hadrian's life by sacrificing his own. Hadrian founded a city in Egypt to honor his companion and had statues of Antinous placed in shrines throughout the empire, much as Livia and later emperors' wives were honored.

Hadrian's devotion to Antinous scandalized Rome. But this emperor was not a creature of the capital, and he felt no obligation to conform to its views. In his life and travels Hadrian aptly represented a diverse empire, where the traditions of Greece, Egypt, and other cultured lands rivaled those of Italy, and where not all roads led to Rome.

Hadrian's beloved Antinous, who drowned in the Nile in AD 130, was glorified after his death as a godlike pharaoh in this sculpture for Hadrian's villa.

ROMAN RETREATS

"You may wonder why my Laurentine place . . . is such a joy to me," Pliny the Younger wrote a friend about his country villa, "but once you realize the attractions of the house itself, the amenities of its situation, and its extensive sea front, you will have your answer." The amenities and attractions of Roman villas were certainly compelling, especially since they usually included a breathtaking view, a spacious house with private baths and flourishing gardens, as well as walls full of artwork.

Wealthy Romans purchased much of Italy's rural land during the Republican period, building retreats to escape city life. The coastal region around Pompeii and Herculaneum proved a popular location for these fabulous country homes. The volcanic eruption that engulfed those cities in AD 79 preserved most of the villas and furnishings pictured here and on the following pages.

A sprawling seaside villa of porticoed walkways and lush gardens dominates its rustic setting in this Pompeian wall painting. Many Romans kept guard dogs for protection at the villas, a fact advertised to would-be intruders by the floor mosaic at left, warning, Beware of Dog.

48

An Elegant Design

Although no two Roman villas were the same, each usually possessed two similar features: an atrium and a peristyle. The atrium, a large room inside the villa's main entrance, served as an entry hall. Its open skylight was also part of a system for catching rainwater to fill the house's cisterns. The atrium led into a colonnaded garden area, the peristyle, which provided greenery and let light into surrounding rooms.

Surprisingly, though well-appointed houses conveyed status, the rooms tended to be small and sparsely furnished. Wealthy Romans spent lavish amounts of money on the furniture they did have, seeking pieces of rare wood, ivory, and gold. Their less fortunate countrymen could have lived well for years on what the rich paid for a single table.

Sunlight, rather than rain, spills through the opening in this atrium's roof, falling on the basin for catching rainwater directly below. Behind the atrium lies the sunny garden area of the peristyle, a courtyard that became the signature feature of the Roman house.

A bedroom in the villa of Publius Fannius Sinistor, with
its spare furnishings and extravagantly decorated walls
and floor, exemplifies the Roman decorating ideal.

THE ART OF DECORATING

Romans decorated almost every room in their villas with murals and mosaics. As a matter of fact, paintings of scenes from nature, figures from mythology, and still lifes adorned the walls of most houses in towns such as Pompeii and Herculaneum. In the villas, however, the displays became much more elaborate, a reflection of both the owner's taste and social status. The most complex and vivid scenes adorned the main rooms, such as the atrium, the dining room, and the master's bedroom. Yet even the slaves' quarters might sport a few small pictures.

As always, styles of artwork varied. Some artists employed tricks of perspective, shading, and foreshortening to conjure up surprisingly realistic vistas that transported the viewer to other locales. Others used stucco reliefs and detailed brushwork to create the appearance of fine polished marble or worked stone on plain plaster walls. To further

The skillful rendering of this town scene *(left)* undoubtedly made viewers from the city feel at home. With similar realism, the painting at right gives the impression that a woman is about to enter the room, an illusion amplified by the addition of a set of real stairs.

A decorative border painted to look like marble from the villa at Oplontis still fools even the most careful observer.

Real seashells frame and enliven this detail from a multicolored wall mosaic found in an alcove of a villa's garden.

transform the villas, mosaicists were brought in to decorate floors and walls with their colorful handiwork, fashioning realistic pictures of flora and fauna or intricate geometric designs.

Although the villas' owners did not wield the paintbrushes or set the colored stones, they undoubtedly chose the subjects to be represented, and their personal interests were clearly reflected on their walls. Scenes of family life appeared, as did depictions of the great villas themselves. An interest in Egypt, which intensified after the Roman annexation of that country in 30 BC, was expressed in renderings of Egyptian landscapes and rituals. Historical and mythological subjects, however, held more fascination for the Romans than any other. And while heroes and deities were usually treated with respect, it was not unknown for sly artists to depict them with a bit of Roman irreverence.

A music instructor teaches his young pupil how to play the cithara in this fanciful scene from a villa in the town of Herculaneum.

Reflecting the Roman interest in Egypt, a mongoose, a cobra, and a hippopotamus share the Nile with a pair of ducks in this stylized mosaic from the House of the Faun *(above)*. A whimsical wall painting from another villa portrays a trio of cupids playing hide-and-seek *(left)*.

A young woman gathers flowers *(below)* and birds perch above a small bubbling fountain *(right)* in these paintings from Roman homes. Fountains sprang up among the greenery in many of Pompeii's gardens following the building of the Augustan aqueduct, which brought running water to the peristyles.

Beauty and serenity are the hallmarks of this faithful re-creation of a Roman peristyle garden and villa, home of the J. Paul Getty Museum in Malibu, California.

GARDENS OF EARTHLY DELIGHT

Romans loved their gardens, and they wanted as many rooms as possible to face the peristyle. Pliny the Younger boasted in a letter to a friend that a dining room overlooking one of his gardens "has a view as lovely as that of the sea itself." Pliny and his guests often ate in the garden, resting their dishes on the edge of a fountain basin while plucking hors d'oeuvres from small boat-shaped plates floating in the water.

While a country villa's garden might be used for cultivating fruit and vegetables, its urban counterpart served a purpose just as important: It offered a glimpse of nature amid the crowded cityscape. So important was the garden to Romans that where a real one could not be maintained, vivid scenes of trees, shrubbery, and flowers were painted on the walls of their homes.

CHAPTER TWO

PROUD ROMANS OF EVERY RANK

Urging his straining oxen on with a goad, a sturdy plowman cuts furrows in a field while a sower broadcasts seed from his basket during the autumn planting season. By the first century AD most agricultural labor was performed for wealthy Roman landowners by tenant farmers, slaves, or other retainers.

ucius Pedanius Secundus was a man of weighty responsibilities. As prefect of Rome during the reign of Nero, he was charged with maintaining order in a city filled to bursting with roughly a million residents. Authorized to punish crimes, the city prefect had command of troops and used them as a police force to keep revelers in line during festivals and games. He and his men were also there to guard against insurrection by Rome's many slaves.

The great city Pedanius Secundus watched over was the pulsing heart of the empire and owed its vitality to the river, roads, and aqueducts that served as its arteries, benefiting rich and poor alike. While only the wealthiest residents had baths in their homes—fed by spurs from the aqueducts or by water drawn by slaves from one of hundreds of fountains or basins around the city—Romans of all classes visited the public baths and frequented public lavatories with running water (a great sewer called the Cloaca Maxima funneled the refuse into the Tiber). Poor Romans whose dingy apartments lacked kitchens could still feast their eyes on fresh produce offered at stalls in the bustling marketplaces and pick up something there for dinner, perhaps, or stop for a bite at one of the many taverns.

For all its attractions, Rome was a dangerous place, and the prefect had much to worry about. The streets were so narrow that all wagons except those carrying building materials were barred from using them before nightfall. Nonetheless, pedestrians who were not careful might still be knocked over in broad daylight by chariots bound for a race at the Circus Maximus, or have their feet trampled by soldiers wearing sharp-studded shoes, or be shoved aside by slaves clearing a path for their noble master, riding above the fray in his litter. Anyone who was foolish enough to venture out alone at night for some refreshment or a rendezvous with one of the city's brightly clad prostitutes ran the risk of being mugged. And staying home after dark did not ensure one's safety, for neither bolts nor guard dogs provided adequate protection against Rome's bold and resourceful burglars.

Wealthy Romans responded to such threats by surrounding themselves with bodyguards. But no one was entirely safe from crime—not even Pedanius Secundus himself. One day in AD 61 Rome's prefect and guardian of public order was found murdered in his home. The identity of the victim was shocking enough, but the circumstances were even more so. He was slain not by some intruding ruffian but by one of his own household slaves.

The motive for the murder remained unclear. Some said that the victim had reneged on a promise to let the slave purchase his freedom for a set price (valued household slaves received occasional tips and presents, and some in positions of responsibility were rewarded by their masters with a *peculium*, or "nest egg"). Others attributed the murder to jealousy, claiming that the prefect had made advances to a man the killer himself was infatuated with. Whatever the provocation, Roman law decreed that the slave

TAMPERING WITH FATE

Two women watch anxiously as an old spell caster *(far right)* recites a charm. Many Romans were convinced that occult powers controlled their lives and practiced magical arts in hopes of altering their own destiny or the fortunes of others. Aside from casting spells, they wrote curse tablets damning their enemies and portrayed phallic symbols and other potent images on walls to promote fertility, propitiate the gods, or ward off evil spirits.

must die for his deed. And he would not be the only one to pay with his life. In such cases all the slaves in the victim's household were considered guilty by association and subject to the death penalty as well. The murdered prefect had a huge retinue of slaves—some 400 men, women, and children.

Whether to execute hundreds for the crime of one man became a matter of intense debate in Rome. Many people thought that a mass execution in this instance would be an outrage, and angry crowds supporting the slaves besieged the Senate when it convened to consider their fate. According to the historian Tacitus, there was some feeling among the senators—most of whom had large numbers of slaves themselves—that the proposed penalty was too sweeping and severe. But Gaius Cassius Longinus, a descendant of the man of that same name who had helped plan the as-

"You have as many enemies as you have slaves."

a population of slaves culled from many alien nations, "The only way to keep down this scum is by intimidation." Yes, innocent people would suffer, he conceded, "but individual wrongs are outweighed by the advantage of the community."

None of the senators opposed his assertions, but the hordes of Romans agitating for clemency had reason to doubt that the executions benefited their community. A few major slave revolts in the past, such as the uprising of the gladiator Spartacus and his followers in 73 BC, had indeed threatened the society at large. But in this case the offense was largely of concern to people of means. "You have as many enemies as you have slaves," went the old saying, and household slaves had access to their masters at the most vulnerable of times. Ruled by their fears, the senators voted to approve the death sentences. An irate mob armed with rocks and

sassination of Julius Caesar, demanded death for all concerned. "Exempt them from penalty if you like," he warned the doubters. "But then, if the City Prefect was not important enough to be immune, who will be? Who will have enough slaves to protect him if Pedanius' four hundred were too few?"

Cassius Longinus scoffed at the idea that the killer could have acted without the knowledge or help of others, "Do you believe that a slave can have planned to kill his master without letting fall a single rash or menacing word? Or even if we assume he kept his secret—and obtained a weapon unnoticed—could he have passed the watch, opened the bedroom door, carried in a light, and committed the murder, without anyone knowing?" The speaker added that stern measures were needed to discipline

torches tried to block the execution, but Nero sent troops to quell the protest, and the condemned were led to their deaths.

For one dignitary named Cingonius Varro, not even the execution of 400 people was sufficient punishment. He wanted the freed slaves who had been serving under the victim's roof at the time of his murder deported. Nero, however, rejected that proposal as unjust. Perhaps this singular act of clemency on his part was meant as a concession to the large Roman population of ex-slaves, or freedmen, some of whom had risen from servitude to become prominent businessmen and imperial administrators. Their success demonstrated that the Roman social order, for all its inequities, afforded opportunities for advancement. The fate of the prefect's slaves dramatized the perils for those at the lowest rungs, but many slaves, ex-slaves, and common citizens found ways of profiting by their talents and raising their status.

It was not just Roman aristocrats who distinguished themselves but people of lowly origins like Tiro—slave to the orator Cicero, who won his freedom by serving brilliantly as his master's confidential secretary—or the poet Horace, a freedman's son who earned support from the rich and powerful in Rome but celebrated in verse the humble virtues of the countryside, as personified by his old neighbor, the tenant farmer Ofellus. Other men and women of plain heritage around the empire made smaller but lasting impressions on posterity by asserting their rights in court or by succeeding in business, like those who made Pompeii such a vibrant place on the eve of the eruption of Mount Vesuvius in AD 79. As their stories confirm, the Roman world was a stage where actors from every walk of life could make the most of their assigned roles or aspire to new ones.

For Cicero and Tiro the ties that bound master to slave could not have been stronger. Raised in the early first century BC in Cicero's house at Arpinum, not far from Rome, Tiro was younger than his master, who belonged to the second level of Rome's elite—the wealthy equestrian order—but used his fortune and his great oratorical skills to rise to senatorial rank and win election as consul. Among the assets that helped Cicero achieve such distinction as a *novus homo,* or "new man," was the gifted Tiro. Early on, someone in the household, perhaps Cicero himself, recognized in the eager slave boy the makings of a good secretary and provided him with instruction. Like Cicero and other upper-class Romans, Tiro became literate in Latin and most likely mastered Greek as well.

As an educated household slave, Tiro fared far better than most others in bondage. There were more

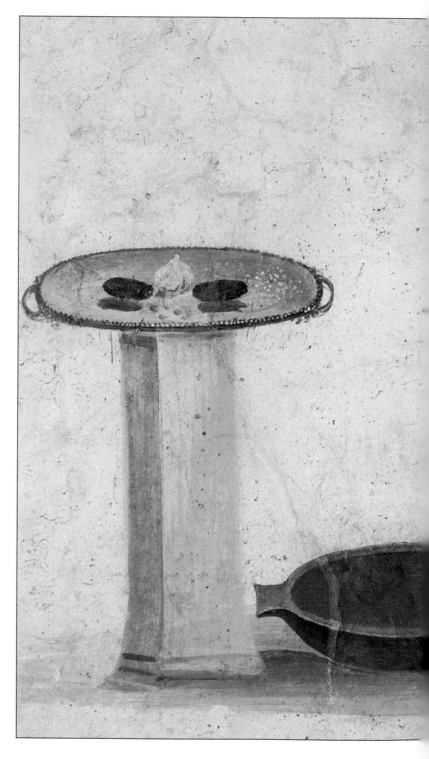

Two slaves dress a fawn for their master's evening meal, richer fare than they themselves will enjoy. Slaves, like other poor Romans, lived largely on grain, supplemented by olives, figs, and other tidbits.

than 100,000 slaves in Rome alone and perhaps as many as two million throughout all of Italy. Few were as fortunate as Cicero's secretary was. Many were born into slavery; others were scooped up as foundlings or were seized by pirates or by conquering Roman armies.

Some slaves performed backbreaking labor in mines or served as oarsmen on merchant ships. Other unfortunates worked for their masters as prostitutes or fighters, powered treadmills or cleaned public buildings, or toiled on rural estates where their rations were measured out as meticulously as feed for the livestock. A treatise on agriculture by Cato the Elder advised estate owners to nourish their slaves on grain or bread, inferior wine from grape skins, and those olives that were not worth pressing for oil. Cato

and our host Xenomenes is as fond of you as though he had been your bosom companion."

As a slave Tiro was defined legally as a *res mancipii,* or "item of purchase," meaning that he could be sold or rented out like other forms of property. His only protection against being bought or borrowed was to make himself indispensable to Cicero, and he did just that by taking on a variety of important tasks. While Cicero busied himself in Rome with a public career that led him to the consulship in 63 BC, Tiro may well have acted as his bookkeeper and helped manage his several country estates. It was as Cicero's secretary, however, that Tiro made his greatest contribution. Using a system of shorthand that he perfected called Tironian notes, he recorded many of Cicero's

"You must shed your town-bred ways— you are now a Roman squire!"

added that masters should retrieve from slaves their old tunics and cloaks, to be made into patchworks. Some slaves were branded by their masters, and others were fitted with iron collars so that they could be identified and returned if they ran away. "I have escaped from my post," read the collar on one Roman slave. "Return me to the barbers' shop near the temple of Flora."

Even household slaves performing congenial tasks in comfortable surroundings sometimes endured shameful treatment, for they had no right to refuse their masters' sexual advances. Slaves with conscientious owners might escape such indignities, but they were still expected to flatter their superiors. Tiro excelled at such courtesies and continued to beguile Cicero and company even after winning his freedom. "What a charmer you are!" Cicero once wrote to him. "We spent two hours at Thyrreum,

remarks and speeches and helped preserve his eloquence in writing. More than a scribe, he served as an editor and adviser to Cicero, who once described the manuscripts they produced as "my (or *our*) literary brain-children."

Perhaps Tiro made himself too valuable to Cicero as a slave, for while the orator often talked of freeing him, that reward was long in coming. It must have been difficult for Tiro to press the matter, for all masters expected *fides,* or selfless loyalty, from their slaves, and Cicero's vanity was such that he saw himself in the best light and expected others to do the same. Could the man who was hailed as the father of his country be anything but a just and generous master?

Yet the fact remained that as Tiro entered his forties, having devoted his life to Cicero, he was still a slave. He had no reason

Clambering inside a treadmill, slaves provide power to operate ropes and pulleys and raise a builder's crane. To discourage such hard-pressed slaves from running away, masters fitted them with collars *(above)* engraved with the owner's name and address. Captured runaways, or *fugitivi*, were branded on the forehead with the letters *FUG*.

Scribes record an orator's speech with styluses in books consisting of a number of wax-covered tablets.

THE TOOLS OF LITERACY

Writing tablets returned with a sorry answer," wrote the poet Ovid after getting a note from his mistress thwarting plans for a tryst. "God rot their wood with worm and their wax with white mildew!" However much he cursed those wax-covered wooden tablets, neither he nor his fellow Romans could function without such writing materials. Theirs was a literate society, and writing pervaded all aspects of life. At work merchants drafted contracts and scribes transcribed legal proceedings. In the streets promoters and political factions adorned city walls with notices and graffiti. At home family members wrote letters and recorded household accounts.

Romans had a variety of writing materials, including Ovid's despised tablets, which could be reused. Writers etched the wax surface with a pointed stylus like the ivory one at right, with a flat end for erasing mistakes and creating a smooth new surface. For letters or records Romans often wrote on papyrus, using a reed or metal pens (right, bottom) dipped in a solution containing octopus ink. Whatever medium a Roman writer chose, readers could face a formidable challenge deciphering the text. There were often no spaces between words, and punctuation marks were scarce.

A young married couple from Pompeii display their love of learning by holding writing implements in this portrait.

This lead curse tablet from Bath, England, casts an evil spell on the man who seduced the writer's sweetheart: "May he who carried off Sylvia from me become as liquid as water. [May] he who obscenely devours her become dumb."

to complain of his surroundings, whether he was minding one of his master's country estates or conferring with Cicero at his gracious townhouse, faced with Greek marble and shaded by elm trees on the fashionable Palatine Hill. Even the best-kept slave, however, labored under a burden of anxiety. What if his master lost his fortune, or came under attack by political opponents? Under Roman law a slave who was called to testify in court could be tortured before being questioned, a measure thought necessary to wring the truth from slaves. Indeed, any master for a fee could have authorities torture or kill one of his slaves and dispose of the body.

A fond master like Cicero would never subject Tiro to such treatment, but the slaves of a kind owner who died or fell into debt might end up in cruel hands. Some masters flogged their slaves for infractions as minor as failing to fetch hot water fast enough. A few sadists delighted in devising novel ways to torture or kill errant slaves. The Roman author Pliny the Elder told of a jaded equestrian named Vedius Pollio who stocked the ponds at his home with flesh-eating lamprey eels and fed to them slaves condemned for one offense or another, simply because he relished seeing a man torn to pieces. Once, while entertaining the emperor Augustus, Pollio ordered a slave boy thrown to the eels for breaking a glass. Disgusted by his host's brutality, Augustus blocked the execution by ordering every glass in the house broken to show that the boy could not be punished for doing as the emperor did.

For Tiro freedom represented not just protection from the random cruelties of slavery but a chance to taste the precious liberty extolled by Cicero and by the earlier Greek and Roman orators he took as his models. Some Romans drew up wills bequeathing the gift of liberty to their slaves, but Tiro had no certainty of outliving his owner and could only hope that Cicero would follow the example of other masters who granted slaves freedom for services rendered. A fertile slave woman, for example, might be emancipated for bearing several sons, who would remain the property of her master after she herself was freed. Surely, Tiro had done enough to warrant a similar reward.

At last Cicero set a date to free Tiro, perhaps prompted by concern for the health of his ailing

A CEASELESS FLOW OF GOODS

"From neighboring continents far and wide a ceaseless flow of goods pours into Rome," enthused a visitor from Greece. "Anything that cannot be seen in Rome does not exist." Merchants imported amber from the Baltic, silk from China, and spices from India, and much of that cargo moved by water.

Barges, like the one below laden with wine, plied the rivers, often rowed or pulled by slaves, while ships, like those with sails lowered in the harbor scene at right, traversed the seas, braving storms and sometimes sinking. The wealthy freedman Trimalchio in Petronius's *Satyricon* told of losing five ships in his first venture. "Do you think that stopped me?" he boasted. "I bought more ships, larger, better, luckier ones... and loaded them again with wine, bacon, fat, beans, perfume and slaves."

slave. "You must get ready to restore your services to my Muses," Cicero wrote encouragingly to the convalescing Tiro in April of 53 BC. "My promise will be performed on the appointed day." A month or two later the orator's younger brother Quintus wrote to congratulate Cicero for freeing Tiro. "Believe me, I jumped for joy," Quintus exulted, after commending Cicero for acknowledging Tiro's "former condition to be below his deserts and preferring us to have him as a friend rather than a slave." Loyalty in a slave was one thing, Quintus went on, but Tiro was to be valued all the more for his "literary accomplishments and conversation and culture."

As a freedman, or *libertus,* Tiro was entitled to Roman citizenship and eligible to own property. However, his fealty to Cicero did not end with his manumission, for Tiro now became Cicero's client, and as such, was expected to show his patron not only fides but other forms of devotion—including *pietas,* or the respect due a father from his son; and perhaps *operae,* or services, in the form of a number of days of work each year. Tiro continued to act as Cicero's secretary and collaborator and likely received financial rewards for his services because he eventually purchased property in the country. Cicero's son, off studying in Athens in 44 BC, wrote Tiro to congratulate him on his acquisition: "You must shed your town-bred ways—you are now a Roman squire!"

Not all freedmen fared so well. Many, liberated not just from slavery but from the comforts of their master's home, could afford nothing better than a cramped apartment in one of Rome's rickety tenements, or *insulae,* up to six stories high and prone to fires and cave-ins. Some freedmen, using skills acquired in bondage, set themselves up as artisans, rented shops on the ground floors of apartment buildings, and lived in the shop or an adjoining room. Tenement dwellers endured stifling heat in the summers and shriveling cold in the winter, moderated only slightly by the

City dwellers of limited means lived in modest houses like the one above in Herculaneum—shared by two families, one on each floor—or occupied larger apartment buildings. In most cases they had to resort to public latrines *(left).*

faint glow of a small charcoal brazier. Plumbing was scarce or nonexistent, and pots of flowers in the few windows were often the sole adornments. Cicero, himself a slumlord, complained to a friend that two of the tenements he owned had collapsed and that others had gaping cracks. Conditions were so bad, he confided, that "not only the tenants, but even the mice have moved out!"

Even after achieving the status of a landowner, Tiro still acknowledged Cicero as his patron. A client owed his patron the honor of hailing him regularly at his home and perhaps forming part of his entourage when he traveled in his litter to the Forum or the Senate. As patron and client, Cicero and Tiro would never be equals, but their relationship was not only cordial but intimate, much like that between a father and son. Cicero once urged the absent Tiro in a letter to take good care of his health "if you love me, and if you don't you make a very pretty pretense of it." Cicero went on to remind Tiro what good health required:

An official measures out free wheat for the needy as more grain arrives. Under Augustus the dole fed as many as 320,000 Romans daily.

Gripping poles and holding hands to keep from slipping, two laborers tread grapes in a shallow vat while a third staggers under a basket brimming with more fruit. Each September, when the grapes were harvested, vineyard owners hired large numbers of temporary workers to augment the regular labor force.

"digestion, no fatigue, a short walk, massage, proper evacuation. Mind you come back in good shape."

Bonds of duty and affection dictated that Tiro would not challenge or embarrass Cicero during his lifetime—no small matter, given Tiro's thorough knowledge of his patron's foibles. Accordingly, Tiro waited until after Cicero's death in 43 BC, by execution at the behest of Mark Antony, to write a biography of the orator. Although Tiro's account was lost, it reportedly dealt more frankly with Cicero's life than his late master might have wished. Yet Tiro had nothing to apologize for. He no longer had

to be slavish in his devotion to Cicero, and he duly honored the orator's memory by publishing a number of his speeches and letters posthumously. Tiro himself lived to the ripe age of 100, it was said, having spent at least half his years as a free man.

Happy is the man who remains far from the world of business," wrote the Roman poet Horace, "and who cultivates the family farm with his own oxen; who refrains from moneylending, who is not a soldier roused from sleep by the harsh trumpet or quaking in terror on a stormy sea; who avoids the Forum and the haughty thresholds of our more important citizens. Instead, he trains the mature tendrils of his grapevines to the tall poplar trees; or he stands in a secluded valley and surveys his herds of lowing cattle as they graze."

This ode to rural pleasures was not quite as idyllic as it seemed, for the character who spoke these lines in Horace's poem was a businessman and money-lender who could afford to visit the country at his leisure, leaving the hard work of tending the land and livestock to others. Horace, writing around 30 BC, knew well that the sturdy farmer celebrated in Roman lore was a vanishing breed. Most of Italy's farmland was now in the hands of wealthy estate owners, like the late Cicero, who spent much of their time in the city and visited their holdings in the country periodically. Horace himself grew up in rural Italy but found his calling in Rome. Born Quintus Horatius Flaccus in 65 BC, he was the son of an ex-slave who acquired some land in Apulia—a fertile region in southern Italy—but made his living chiefly as a public auctioneer, collecting goods from people who fell into debt and had to sell their property.

Horace's father made enough from other's misfortunes to provide his son with a fine education, and his future looked bright. While studying in Greece, however, Horace met Marcus Brutus, who had fled Rome after the assassination of Julius Caesar. Horace sided with Brutus in the struggle that ended at Philippi in 42 BC with Brutus's defeat and suicide. Afterward the land Horace's father had acquired was con-

fiscated as part of an effort by Octavian and his fellow triumvirs to reward their supporters, often at the expense of their opponents. Horace went to Rome, where he was lucky to find work as an official clerk. In time his literary talents won him entry to the circle of the hugely wealthy Gaius Maecenas, who had close ties to Octavian and had profited when Octavian's opponents were stripped of their assets. Maecenas patronized the epic poet Virgil and other brilliant writers, regardless of their political background, and restored Horace as a man of property by granting him a country estate.

Horace had no illusions about what it took to live at ease in the country. Only a wealthy Roman—or one with a generous patron like Maecenas—could afford to enjoy days of quiet contemplation amid haystacks, beehives, and babbling streams. All others who hoped to survive in rural Italy had to work hard, and not many of them were their own masters. Most agricultural labor was performed by slaves, hired help, tenant farmers, or sharecroppers.

By the late first century BC, many estate owners were turning away from slave labor for economic reasons. Grain and other agricultural goods were pour-

A silver figurine evoking rural charms shows a shepherd bearing a lamb in a sling, artfully balanced by the weight of a jug.

ing into Italy from North Africa and other fertile places under Roman rule. Some of that grain was free—provided by subject provinces as tribute—and the imports lowered prices. In lean times slaves still had to be fed and clothed at the owner's expense, while hired help could be laid off and tenants could be required to pay their rents or face eviction. Tenant farmers often had the additional duty of providing services for their landlord and patron by working a few days a year for him without pay. Nonetheless, some farmers who had lost their land recently through debt or confiscations preferred to work the soil for others rather than move to the city and join the crowds there queuing up for free grain, doled out to prevent unrest.

Among those who chose to remain in the country as a tenant farmer was Ofellus, described by Horace as an old neighbor of his in Apulia. Ofellus had once owned the land he farmed, but his property was taken from him and assigned to a veteran named Umbrenus, probably as part of the same confiscation that cost Horace's family their land. Ofellus stayed on the property as a tenant of the new owner. To Horace he embodied rural virtues. In one of his poems Horace praised Ofellus as "a philosopher unschooled and of rough mother-wit," and offered him as a model of thrift and fortitude in trying circumstances: "You may see him on his little farm, now assigned to others, with his cattle and his sons, a sturdy tenant farmer, and this is his story."

City dwellers who wasted their health and wealth at the banquet table, Horace noted, would do well to heed Ofellus, who was "not the man to eat on a working day, without good reason, anything more than greens and the shank of a smoked ham." And just because he was thrifty did not mean he was stingy. When guests arrived, Ofellus offered "a pullet or a kid" fresh from his yard, followed by a plain but tasty dessert of "raisins and nuts and split figs." What more was needed than this, and a little wine, to smooth out "the worries of a wrinkled brow"?

As a poet, Horace was little concerned with the mundane labors that allowed Ofellus and family to meet their simple needs. Land had to be plowed and manured, seeds sown and rows hoed, plots weeded and watered. Then there were animals to be fed, milked, and foaled, and in harvesttime, crops to be gathered, hay made, grapes squeezed, olives pressed, and grain ground. Nor did the short, wet Mediterranean winter provide rest for the weary, for there were fences to mend and roofs to repair. Most Roman farmers tried to leave part of their land fallow periodically. The resources of both the soil and the farmers must have been strained to the limit, however, when tenants had to make their rent. Ofellus and others in his position could sympathize with the farmer's lament, "From the day of my birth I have lived by working my land; neither my land nor I has ever had a rest."

Perhaps the real Ofellus was less content with his lot than the man portrayed by Horace. But the poet knew what it was like to be dispossessed, and he admired the tenacity and forbearance that kept farmers like Ofellus attached to their land and their occupation, even if others reaped the benefits. "Today the land bears the name of Umbrenus; of late it had that of Ofellus; to no one will it belong for good," concluded Horace. "Live, then, as brave men, and with brave hearts confront the strokes of fate."

All around the Roman Empire there were countless men and women like Ofellus, people who might be free under the law but who had to toil for others at a disadvantage. They were not entirely at the mercy of their landlords or employers, however. Some worked under contracts that spelled out what was expected of them, and what they were owed in return. The terms might not be generous, but they were legally binding, and tenants and employees could appeal to the courts if they thought that a contract was being violated, just as their bosses could. Such disputes were usually resolved by magistrates, who were supposed to rule impartially, based on the terms of the contract and on sound legal precedents.

One intriguing case of this kind came before a Roman magistrate in Egypt in AD 49, some 80 years after Octavian claimed the land. An advocate representing a man of means named Pesuris brought a complaint against a woman called Saraeus. Pesuris had taken "a male child from the dunghill," the advocate attested, and had then hired Saraeus to serve as the child's *nutrix,* or wet-nurse. In many parts of the Roman world, parents left unwanted infants in desolate places to die

A nursemaid tenderly cradles a young child clutching at her breast. Mothers or caretakers who were unable to breast-feed, or weary of it, might use a feeding bottle *(below)*. The historian Tacitus criticized the practice of letting servants or slaves raise a youngster of noble birth, who grew up "steeped in their ignorant stories and lies."

or be taken up by others, usually as slaves. Pesuris contracted with Saraeus to nurse this particular foundling, dubbed Heraclas, evidently hoping that the boy would thrive and return the investment as a slave.

Saraeus was a free woman, but she must have been in considerable financial need to accept this job, for the wages offered a wet-nurse were low, and a nursing contract might contain conditions that were strict and intrusive. Some contracts prohibited sexual intercourse by the nurse, for example, on the grounds that it would lessen her affection for the child or spoil her milk. There were few requirements for the job other than the ability to nurse a baby. Saraeus qualified on that count, for she had just weaned a boy of her own. Although slave women sometimes served as nurses, it was not strictly a menial task. Nurses in Roman society not only relieved wealthy women of the burden of breast-feeding—a task some considered beneath their dignity—but often went on to serve as nannies or governesses of the children they weaned.

Saraeus, however, was engaged just as a wet-nurse. She contracted to nurture the infant Heraclas in her home for two years, and all seemingly went well. It was only after she returned the boy to Pesuris that trouble arose. One day, Pesuris's advocate told the magistrate, Saraeus burst into his client's house and took the child. The only defense she offered for her action, according to the advocate, was that the boy was not a slave at all but free.

This apparent mystery was cleared up in court by Saraeus herself, who testified on her own behalf (she probably could not afford an advocate). The boy Heraclas had died in her care, she confessed, which meant that she had to return to Pesuris the balance of the wages she had received from him in advance. Apparently, she and her husband could not afford to do so, for they

Nursemaids and governesses tried to keep children out of each other's hair *(top right)* by diverting them with toys such as the rag doll and marbles shown here.

concealed the death of Heraclas and replaced him with their own little boy when the time was up. That child was older than Heraclas, but Pesuris had no reason to complain if Saraeus returned to him a child who was larger and stronger than expected—so much the better from the master's point of view. After parting with her natural child, Saraeus evidently had misgivings and snatched him back. "Now they are trying to take my own boy from me," she testified plaintively.

The magistrate was no Solomon, but he did reach a decision that offered something to both parties. The boy in question was present in the courtroom, and he looked to the magistrate to be Saraeus's child. If she and her husband would swear that Heraclas had in fact died in their care, he ruled, they could keep their boy, provided that they repaid to Pesuris the money they owed him.

Pesuris may have been disappointed by this ruling, for the boy was surely worth more to him as a slave than what little he would recoup from Saraeus. But the judge saw no reason to compensate him for his unlucky investment in the ill-fated Heraclas. As for Saraeus, she might be poor and imprudent, but she was still free and entitled to certain rights, the judge concluded, and so was her son.

Aside from slaves, everyone in Roman society had a certain standing under the law. To be sure, those in disreputable trades such as prostitution had fewer rights than others. Prostitutes could not marry men who were free citizens by birth, for example, and the law did not allow them the same protection against harassment accorded other free women. Nonetheless, magistrates sometimes made significant legal concessions to prostitutes—or at least to their customers. Prostitutes were exempted from the laws against adultery imposed by Augustus, for example.

In one celebrated court case a prostitute by the name of Manilia took on one of Rome's leading officials and won. That dignitary,

Aulus Hostilius Mancinus, wanted to bring charges before a jury against the prostitute for injuring him with a stone outside her establishment one night. In order to do so, however, he first had to make his case to Rome's tribunes, who held veto power over prosecutions they deemed unwarranted. Mancinus had a wound to show as evidence, and he even had a plausible excuse for visiting Manilia's apartment. In his official capacity as an aedile, he kept an eye on prostitutes and perhaps had the right to inspect their premises.

But the prostitute Manilia was allowed a say in the proceedings as well, and she offered the tribunes a far different view of what Mancinus was up to that night. She testified that he had come to her home dressed not in his official robes but in his "party clothes," including a festive garland around his brow, suggesting that he was looking for a good time. As it happened, she was otherwise occupied at the time, and it was not "convenient" for her to let him in. He then tried to force his way into her apartment, and she drove him off with stones.

The tribunes agreed with her that there was no

Scantily clad Roman women exercise at the baths before entering the water. To protect their feet, bathers often wore sandals like those on the sign below, wishing newcomers a good bath.

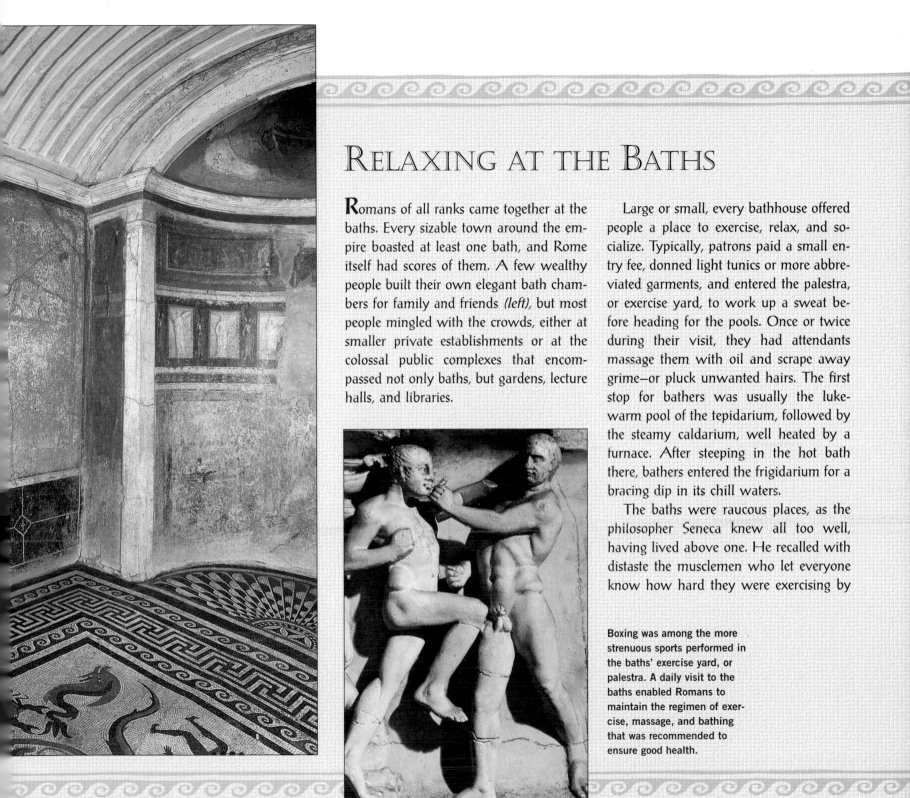

Relaxing at the Baths

Romans of all ranks came together at the baths. Every sizable town around the empire boasted at least one bath, and Rome itself had scores of them. A few wealthy people built their own elegant bath chambers for family and friends *(left)*, but most people mingled with the crowds, either at smaller private establishments or at the colossal public complexes that encompassed not only baths, but gardens, lecture halls, and libraries.

Large or small, every bathhouse offered people a place to exercise, relax, and socialize. Typically, patrons paid a small entry fee, donned light tunics or more abbreviated garments, and entered the palestra, or exercise yard, to work up a sweat before heading for the pools. Once or twice during their visit, they had attendants massage them with oil and scrape away grime—or pluck unwanted hairs. The first stop for bathers was usually the lukewarm pool of the tepidarium, followed by the steamy caldarium, well heated by a furnace. After steeping in the hot bath there, bathers entered the frigidarium for a bracing dip in its chill waters.

The baths were raucous places, as the philosopher Seneca knew all too well, having lived above one. He recalled with distaste the musclemen who let everyone know how hard they were exercising by

Boxing was among the more strenuous sports performed in the baths' exercise yard, or palestra. A daily visit to the baths enabled Romans to maintain the regimen of exercise, massage, and bathing that was recommended to ensure good health.

This steaming pool in the Roman town of Bath, England—so named for its soothing waters—was fed by hot mineral springs. At other baths in the empire, a furnace circulated hot air under the floors and through the walls to warm chambers and pools.

emitting loud groans. Adding to the din, he noted, was "a quarrelsome drunk, or sometimes a thief caught in the act, or a man who loves to sing in the bath." Worse still was the "hair plucker, with his shrill and high-pitched voice, continually shrieking in order to be noticed." He was never quiet, Seneca complained, except when he was "plucking armpits and forcing his customer to shriek instead."

Most Romans loved the pools and their clamor, however, and they regarded the big public baths as among the greatest achievements of the rulers who built them. The poet Martial summed up that sentiment after the death of one of Rome's more notorious emperors, "What was worse than Nero? What was better than Nero's hot baths!"

Bath attendants used scented oil from a flask *(far left)* to rub people down, and wielded strigils *(near left)* to scrape away oil and dirt.

good reason for Mancinus to be calling on her at night in such informal attire. They threw out his case and upheld Manilia's right to refuse entry to a man wearing a garland, whatever his rank.

Romans seeking to better their lot found opportunities not only in Rome but in scores of smaller cities that pulsed with their own vitality. Just 130 miles southeast of Rome, for example, lay Pompeii, home in AD 79 to at least 10,000 people. Nestled below Mount Vesuvius and surrounded by fertile fields and pastures, Pompeii took in wool, olives, and grapes from the countryside and turned out cloth, oil, and wine. A major earthquake had rocked the city in AD 62, damaging homes, public buildings, and the water system. A number of wealthy Pompeians had abandoned their homes afterward in favor of lavish new villas along the coast, but other residents stayed put and took part in the city's revival. Some enterprising tradesmen bought or rented the abandoned houses and converted them into workshops.

Pompeii was girded by high walls and linked to the outside world by eight gates. Docks along the Sarno River received ships from the nearby Bay of Naples. To

A scene embossed on a silver bucket shows a servant brushing a woman's hair as others oil and massage her. The rich often took slaves with them to the baths.

enter the city on the weekly market day was to witness Pompeii at its most colorful. People passing through the gates encountered an array of inns, taverns, and brothels. Some visitors might linger there, but most people here on business would continue down the main thoroughfares past shops and eating houses that catered to the crowds pacing the raised sidewalks (much appreciated in rainstorms, when water streamed down the avenues).

Throughout Pompeii, whitewashed walls provided a backdrop for political endorsements and commercial notices, many of them inscribed by the city's sure-handed *scriptores,* or sign painters. "FOR RENT from July 1," read one notice, "streetfront shops with counter space, luxurious second-story apartments, and a townhouse." Such advertisements vied for wall space with graffiti. "This is no place for idlers," one property owner

warned passersby. "On your way, loafer." Other writers pledged devotion to their sweethearts or scolded philanderers such as one Restitutus, who had allegedly "deceived many girls many times." One wit expressed his low opinion of the graffiti writers as a group: "I wonder, O wall, that you have not fallen in ruins from supporting the stupidities of so many scribblers."

In AD 79 Pompeii was still restoring its forum, badly damaged by the earthquake of 62. Here as in other Roman cities, the forum was the center of public life—a bustling square, surrounded by temples, law courts, and other proud structures. Even as the restoration was proceeding, one corner of the forum served as the marketplace, with porticoes sheltering food stalls and a moneychanger's booth. Merchants and shoppers haggled in the crowded mall. Among the attractions was a domed building with

A woman serves wine to a tavern patron while a dog begs for food. To suit Roman tastes, she would have diluted the wine and then heated it on the raised hearth behind her, stacked with pots.

Romans in search of a meal could wander into one of the many street-side *thermopolia*, or "hot spots," offering warm food and drink, like this one in Ostia. Proprietors inscribed their regular menu on stones like the one below, which offers chicken, fish, ham, and bread.

a tank in the middle—filled with live fish, most likely, so that customers could carry their pick home fresh.

Pompeii was as much a city of scents as of sights. Sea breezes wafted the fragrance of roses from the many gardens through the streets, mingling with the aroma of bread from the bakeries, the smell of rancid bran dumped into the streets for the pigs, the heady bouquet of wine emanating from the vintners, and the tang of *garum,* the fermented fish sauce favored in the taverns and eating houses. But one distinctive odor dominated the rest in certain areas—the insistent smell of urine, used with other ingredients as a detergent to wash wool in the dozen or so fulleries that washed new cloth and laundered dirty garments.

The city's largest fullery was located on the Via Mercurio, just north of the forum, in what had once been a private home. Some evidence suggests that the owner of this establishment was Lucius Veranius Hypsaeus, one of the city's leading businessmen and politicians. Fulleries catered to the desire of Romans to be neatly attired. Plain citizens wore togas that were off-white (the color of natural wool) but still needed cleaning periodically. Men of high status who aspired to public office wore togas that were pure white and had to be laundered frequently. Togas were a staple of the fullers' trade because most homes lacked the space or equipment to launder so large and heavy a

Cheered on by others, two men gamble in a tavern, a popular spot for throwing dice like those below, cast from the cup. Despite periodic attempts to outlaw wagering with dice, betting on cockfights *(above)*, and other gambling, people throughout the empire remained devoted to such contests.

garment—up to 20 feet by 10 feet. People also sent smaller articles such as tunics to the fullers, if they could afford it. Just to have a tunic cleaned might cost as much as four sesterces—a day's pay to a laborer. Fullers in wool-producing areas like Pompeii also kept busy washing wool cloth fresh from the loom, which had to be cleansed of oil and dirt and otherwise prepared for tailoring.

Hypsaeus—or whoever owned the big fullery—had his work cut out for him and wasted no time in getting to it. Like much of Pompeii, he would have risen at dawn and hurried to his place of business, where he greeted his staff of perhaps two dozen employees, some of them freeborn, others slaves or ex-slaves, including children serving as apprentices.

The owner had refurbished the building on the Via Mercurio to make it suitable as a fullery by installing big soaking-and-rinsing tubs, somewhat smaller treading vats, frames for bleaching the fabric, and a press for ironing. Perhaps to enlighten his customers or his new employees as to the business at hand, he had the various steps in the fulling process painted on a wall of the building.

As revealed there in pictures, the first task was to wash the cloth in the treading vats, filled with hot water and detergent. Workers used their feet as agitators, trampling the fabric like grapes at a winery. The urine used in the detergent was collected in jars from the obliging employees and from male passersby (who knew that this was one place where they were always welcome to relieve themselves). It was then mixed with potash, carbonate of soda, and fuller's earth, a kind of absorbent clay, to form a caustic detergent; unfortunately, the mixture also exposed the workers to skin ailments.

After washing, the fabric was steeped in the big rinsing vats, wrung out, and dried. Fabrics that required bleaching were then placed on a conical frame over a smudge pot of burning sulfur, whose fumes constituted yet another health hazard for the workers. The cloth was combed when dry with a brushlike carding tool to raise the nap, which was then sheared off, leaving a smooth surface. Finally, the fabric was pressed in a vise in order to remove wrinkles.

A worker at a fullery tramples wool cloth in a vat containing a cleanser made of urine and other substances to remove the dirt and grease.

The fullers carried out their trade under the divine patronage of Minerva, goddess of wisdom and ingenuity, sometimes represented by an owl, a creature sacred to her. The fullers may also have had an earthly patroness in the form of a woman named Eumachia, the widow of a man in the wool trade and daughter of a brick magnate, who used part of the fortune she inherited to fund construction of an ornate structure at one corner of the forum known as the Building of Eumachia. The fullers honored her there with a statue, and the building may have served as the headquarters of the *collegium,* or guild, to which both the fullers and the wool traders belonged.

Theirs was not the only guild in town. The carpenters, the plumbers, and other groups of tradesmen formed their own collegia for social and political purposes. Members of a guild often threw their collective support behind a particular candidate for public office, hoping no doubt that the man so favored would serve their interests if he won. "The fullers ask you to elect Holconius Priscus," read one sign touting a candidate for duumvir, the highest office in town, shared by two men. (Hypsaeus himself served as duumvir.)

A painting from Pompeii's largest fullery shows an employee carding cloth to raise the nap for shearing while another prepares to bleach fabric on a wicker frame topped by an owl, symbol of the fullers' patron goddess, Minerva. At left, a woman inspects a garment that has been cleaned for her.

Men also formed associations for other purposes, including the funding of proper funerals for the dues-paying members. Then as now, some of these clubs may have had odd titles. One candidate for office in Pompeii received hearty endorsements on the walls from groups identifying themselves as the "petty thieves," the "late drinkers," and the "late sleepers." Perhaps these were genuine endorsements from associations with irreverent names, but more likely they were jibes at the candidate and his supporters by the opposition.

It was only a short distance from the big fullery to the Building of Eumachia, and the owner may often have walked there or to some other gathering place to chat with his colleagues and competitors. There were other diversions to compete for his notice or the attention of his workers, including gladiatorial bouts in Pompeii's amphitheater, which was large enough to accommodate the city's entire population and then some. But when the workday ended—usually by early afternoon, after six hours or so of toil—there was no place more attractive to workers who had been inhaling sulfurous fumes or enduring other travails than the baths, with their inviting pools of hot and cold water.

Both of Pompeii's public baths had been damaged in the big earthquake, and only one of them, the Forum Baths, had been fully repaired. A newer facility, the Central Baths, was under construction, but in the meantime at least some Pompeians were visiting smaller, privately owned baths like the one advertised on

ute to Venus by visiting one of Pompeii's many brothels. But chances are that they popped in more often at one of the city's ubiquitous taverns—just about every block had at least one—for a cup of hot wine, with a bowl of savory lentil stew on the side, perhaps. Then if they had time to kill and money to venture, they probably joined their drinking companions in rolling the dice—a passion that Pompeians shared with Romans everywhere.

Win or lose, the workers and their boss had reason to feel blessed. Their busy little city had many of the advantages of Rome, without the congestion and fuss. It seemed that Venus was taking good care of Pompeii and her people. But fate could be fickle, as those who had lived through the last big earthquake could testify. As it turned out, that convulsion was just a hint of the fury awaiting Pompeii and nearby settlements.

"All were silent . . ."

a wall in Pompeii: "FOR RENT, from August 13, with a 5-year lease on the property of Julia Felix, daughter of Spurius: the elegant Venus Baths, street-front shops and booths, and second-story apartments."

Like Eumachia, the owner of this property was a woman of means. (Some women in Roman society inherited sizable fortunes from their deceased fathers or husbands and might own businesses or offer patronage to clients.) The title of Julia Felix's establishment, Venus Baths, was fitting, for Venus was the patron goddess of Pompeii, and she was honored there in various ways. Sculpted and painted phalli adorned Pompeii's fountains and walls and protruded from doorways. No one considered them indecent in a city ruled by the goddess of love.

Now and then on their way home from the baths, perhaps, fullery workers who could afford it may have paid personal trib-

In August of AD 79 the earth shook again, and the tremors continued ominously for several days. Then on the 24th, Vesuvius erupted, disgorging a vast plume of pumice and ash that descended like a plague on the people in the streets and at home. Slaves and citizens, rich and poor, native born and foreigner—all perished as one in a deluge of volcanic debris that buried their communities, thus preserving the remains for posterity.

Among the testaments that were unearthed at Pompeii in later times was an incomplete line of verse from the poet Virgil, scribbled on a wall by someone who was about to die, perhaps, and who had time only to write these words: "All were silent . . ." The message serves as a haunting epitaph for a city that once resounded with life and that, even in the deathly silence of its ruins, speaks eloquently of the collective accomplishments of the Roman people.

Working for a Living

"Everything that is honorable," wrote the great Roman statesman and orator Cicero in the first century BC, "has its source in the four elements: the first learning, the second sociability, the third greatness of spirit, and the fourth moderation." Cicero suggested that these criteria should pertain to all facets of an individual's life, but perhaps nowhere more than in the pursuit of gainful employment.

Cicero divided occupations into three major categories. The first group included professions that "require greater good sense or else procure substantial benefit, for example medicine, architecture, or teaching." The next, consisting of jobs that Cicero considered "demeaning," were those of tradesmen, handcraftsmen, and merchants. The group Cicero deemed "least worthy of approval" catered to the senses: purveyors of food, such as fishmongers, butchers, and cooks, and entertainers, dancers, and actors.

All Romans did not share Cicero's opinions of trade. On the pitcher above, the god Vulcan is shown hammering at an anvil. And at right, a shipwright's gravestone declares his pride in his profession—it is inscribed "Publius Longidienus hastens to get on with his work."

HONORABLE PROFESSIONS

When Cicero wrote that agriculture was man's most noble occupation, he had in mind wealthy landowners like himself—not peasant farmers who toiled in the fields. If forced to earn a living, though, Cicero asserted that a man could achieve respectability by using good sense to effect good works. He acknowledged that the labors of lawyers, doctors, teachers, and architects benefited society.

A few of these trades could bring great wealth. But many "honorable" occupations paid no more than unskilled jobs, and some professionals were stigmatized for being foreigners or ex-slaves. Caesar tried to reward the skill and public service of the many Greek physicians by granting them citizenship. Yet doctors, who were ineffectual against scourges like smallpox and plague, were not highly regarded by other Romans, including Pliny the Elder, who quipped, "A physician is the only man who can kill anyone with sovereign impunity."

Forceps, used here to remove an arrow from a man's thigh, were common tools of the medical profession, as were the bleeding cup and box of herbal remedies *(above and right).*

Schoolmasters often taught in cramped rooms for little pay. Unlike the Greeks, Romans rarely valued learning for its own sake—only for its practical uses.

"There is no kind of gainful employment that is better, more fruitful, more pleasant and more worthy of a free man than agriculture."

ARTISANS AND TRADESMEN

Upper-class tastes, along with the purchasing power of soldiers home from foreign campaigns, created a demand in Rome for a wide array of goods——from furnishings and building supplies to jewelry and exotic perfumes. Eventually even essential items such as clothing were made, not at home, but in the small shops called tabernae that sprang up around the city center.

Most artisans were semiskilled slaves and freedmen, living and working in the tabernae; others were pieceworkers in large factories. Master craftsmen were in short supply, and the finest of them traveled from job to job. Little distinction was made, however, between a silversmith casting a sculpture and an ironsmith hammering pots, for while the product might be prized, the craftsman was not. Indeed, credit for a work of art went solely to the person who commissioned and paid for it.

Shoemakers specialized in certain products; the cobbler above made only leather boots. Others fashioned ladies' slippers, or shoes and sandals like those at left.

With a hammer and chisel, Icarus, son of Daedalus, legendary inventor of carpentry, cuts mortises at a woodworker's bench.

Seated at a worktable with his wife, a potter or vase painter applies glaze to a pot.

*"All handcraftsmen are engaged in a demeaning trade;
for there can be nothing well bred about the workshop."*

> *"Those who buy from merchants and sell again immediately should also be thought of as demeaning themselves. For they would make no profit unless they told sufficient lies . . ."*

Knife maker and merchant Cornelius Atimetus, on the right, shows a customer some samples of his cutlery.

While the owner looks on, clerks in a fabric-and-cushion shop present a finished pillow to their seated clients.

CATERING TO THE SENSES

Although plowing and planting might be noble occupations, selling the fruits of the harvest was contemptible, by Cicero's stringent standards. Butchers, poultrymen, cooks, fishermen, and fishmongers all received the statesman's disapproval for attending to the pleasures of man. Cicero's fellow nobles had no reservations about availing themselves of such services, however. Even those not wealthy enough to have a staff of slaves could afford to have their meals catered.

But while disdainful of retail grocers and cooked-food vendors, Cicero did make exception for wholesale traders, who performed the honorable civic duty of importing staples like wheat, oil, meat, and wine from Africa, Egypt, and Spain. And though performers and dancers were included in this disreputable group, prostitutes were not—perhaps because they were beneath mentioning. Yet some nobles profited by hiring out slaves in brothels.

Bakers provided most Romans with their daily bread, often in loaves shaped like this one from Pompeii.

Fishermen prepare to cast their net for delicacies highly prized by the upper class: fish and eels.

A selection of produce and live and fresh-killed poultry and rabbits tempt customers who may have been lured to the vendor's stand by the monkeys sitting on the counter.

"The crafts that are least worthy of approval are those that minister to the pleasures."

CHAPTER THREE

FIGHTING IN THE ARMY OF CAESAR

Soldiers subdue naked barbarians in an idealized battle scene carved on a Roman sarcophagus. Captives like the two men crouching at lower right were often enslaved by Roman conquerors. Julius Caesar once auctioned off more than 50,000 captives to slave dealers in one lot.

n a late summer day in 55 BC, a fleet commanded by Julius Caesar approached the steep chalk cliffs of Dover to land Roman troops on the shores of Britain for the first time. Among the vessels were sleek warships—galleys propelled into battle by oarsmen—and 80 bulky transports, traveling under sail and packed with some 8,000 soldiers of the 7th and 10th Legions. These rugged legionaries had campaigned widely under Caesar in recent years, primarily against the Gauls in the region of modern-day France. Although regarded by the Romans as barbarians, the resourceful and well-armed Gauls had sorely tested Caesar's troops. Nothing he had subjected his men to on the Continent, however, quite prepared them for this daring venture. They were soldiers, not sailors, and the waters they were crossing were treacherous. Mercifully, the weather was good, but the men had been aboard the creaking transports for more than eight hours since leaving the coast of France the night before, and the discomforts of the journey were compounded by thoughts of strange and unknowable enemies on the far shore.

Not until Caesar surveyed the cliffs of Dover from his command galley did he know for certain that the Britons, people of the same Celtic heritage as the defiant Gauls, intended to oppose his landing in earnest. Earlier that summer, alarmed by reports that the Romans were assembling a fleet, Britons had dispatched envoys to Caesar, pledging peace and submission. In response Caesar had sent an envoy of his own back with them to Britain to inform tribes there of his impending arrival and to urge them to "entrust themselves to the protection of Rome," as he put it. Well aware that the Britons might not yield without a fight, he proceeded with plans for an armed reconnaissance before the summer was out, to be followed later by a more extensive campaign, if necessary. A successful expedition to remote Britain would significantly bolster his reputation in Rome, where he had yet to attain the supreme authority he would exercise in later years. Yet the risks of the landing were as great as any potential rewards. As Caesar stood on the deck of his galley, he could see enemy warriors massed atop the cliffs, ready to shower missiles down on anyone who set foot on the narrow beach below.

Caesar waited for the rest of his ships to come up, and then the fleet moved with the wind and tide along the coast for several miles to a point where the cliffs receded and the beach sloped gently down to the water. At least his troops would not be pelted from on high there, but the prospects were far from inviting. Awaiting the Romans on shore were fearsome Britons with long hair and mustaches, their bodies painted blue for battle. Some were on horseback and others rode two-man chariots. To reach those determined enemies, the soldiers first had to descend from their transports into the surf and struggle to the shingle

Roman warships armed with bronze-plated beaks to ram enemy ships prepare for battle. Unlike the galleys shown here, conveying troops to board enemy vessels, the warships used by Julius Caesar in his expedition to Britain carried archers and artillerists to support soldiers going ashore.

A standard-bearer holds high the eagle, emblem of Roman might. Each legion had an *aquilifer*, or eagle bearer, who carried the cherished standard into battle.

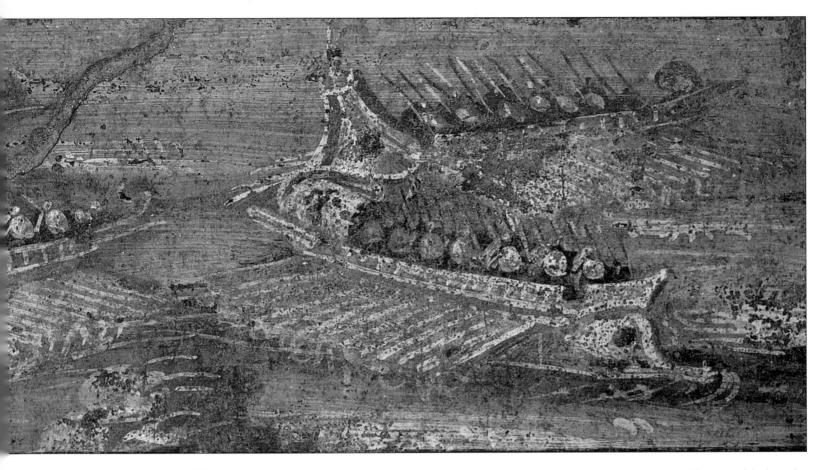

beach under the weight of their armor and weapons, including swords, daggers, and javelins. As Caesar wrote later in his account of the campaign, the perils of the landing "frightened our soldiers, who were unaccustomed to battles of this kind, with the result that they did not show the same alacrity and enthusiasm as they usually did in battles on dry land."

To support the soldiers and spur them on, Caesar directed the warships to sweep around to the left and assail the Britons on their exposed right flank. Pulling in unison, the oarsmen drove the prows of their galleys up onto the beach, allowing the troops on deck to take dead aim at the defenders on shore. Archers unleashed a hail of arrows at the startled defenders, while slingers flung pellets or stones weighing nearly a pound

toward the Britons with deadly velocity. Artillerists added to the barrage by firing catapults that sent larger missiles hurtling toward the enemy with superhuman force, smashing through shields and helmets.

The Britons fell back under the assault, but the soldiers in the transports still hesitated. It remained to the senior standard-bearer of the 10th Legion to set an example for the rest. The eagle standard he carried into battle was sacred to the troops. "Jump down, comrades, unless you want to surrender our eagle to the enemy," he shouted. "I, at any rate, mean to do my duty to my country and my general." So saying, he leaped into the water and waded toward the enemy, with the eagle raised high.

Roused by his words and eager to protect their standard, soldiers all around dropped into the surf and headed for the beach. As they struggled ashore, Britons galloped up and attacked them before they could gain a foothold. Unable to maintain their ranks, soldiers from various units huddled together and fended off the enemy thrusts as best they could. Surveying the confusion on the beach, Caesar sent boats to ferry fresh troops to the spots where the fighting was thickest. At last the Romans had enough men ashore to mount a concerted charge, and they swept the Britons from the beach.

Exhausted and wet, Caesar's troops had little chance to savor their historic landing. Their position was tenuous, and the outcome of their expedition remained very much in doubt. Indeed, they would make little headway in the days to come. Conspicuously absent from Caesar's force was his cavalry, which embarked four days after the rest of the fleet and was driven back to the Continent by storm winds. That same storm came close to stranding the entire force by damaging his ships.

Seeing the Romans at a disadvantage, the Britons laid plans to renew hostilities. By now, however, the invaders they hoped to oust had solidified their position. The first task of the soldiers after seizing their beachhead had been to lay out a camp. Typically, Roman troops built a square camp and reinforced the perimeter by digging a ditch and piling up the loose earth to form an embankment, topped by a palisade of sharpened stakes. This was hard work for battle-weary soldiers, but they were used to it: Romans on the march built such camps routinely at the close of each day. Caesar's troops occupied their camp for some time and may have transformed it into more of a fort than the typical overnight bivouac.

After building up the perimeter, the troops pitched their leather tents in precise order. A broad street separated one legion from another, and a second avenue ran perpendicular to it, forming a T; near the intersection stood the quarters of the commander and his officers. Once Caesar's men had completed their camp, all but the sentries could take to their tents for the night secure in the knowledge that they had raised a rampart against the barbarians.

The Britons were in no hurry to attack the Roman camp. Instead, they lay in wait for the legionaries sent to forage for food. Some time after the storm, while others were repairing the damaged ships, men of the 7th Legion ventured out to cut wheat in some nearby fields cultivated by the Britons and came under heavy assault. Only prompt ac-

OUTFITTED FOR BATTLE

Protective gear worn by Roman troops evolved during the time of the early emperors. Helmets were reinforced with a peak at the brow and a larger neck guard in back to protect against blows, as seen on the helmet at lower right, worn by a cavalryman in the first century AD. And the heavy chain mail tunic of Caesar's day was replaced by plate armor *(shown in replica below)*, which was flexible and allowed for ease of movement. Unchanging were the soldiers' sandals that had iron studs on the soles to withstand miles of marching, thigh-length tunics, and cloaks like the one depicted on the officer at left.

tion by Caesar, who hurried to the scene with reinforcements, prevented a catastrophe. Then, a few days later, Britons launched an unsuccessful attack on the camp itself. Amid persistent hostility, Caesar recognized the danger of remaining in Britain with winter and its storms approaching and safe passage across the channel in doubt. So he concluded a peace with the enemy and set sail with his army back to the Continent in his patched-up vessels while the weather remained favorable.

Caesar soon began planning for a full-scale assault on Britain the following summer. A spectacular fleet of 800 ships carried five legions and 2,000 cavalrymen across the channel. Caesar and his forces beat back stiff challenges from the Britons and made considerable progress, but at summer's end they still faced strong opposition. Once again Caesar accepted peace offers from the Britons and withdrew rather than risk wintering on hostile ground with the stormy channel at his back and restive Gauls threatening trouble on the Continent.

Caesar did not return to Britain, and almost a century would pass before Roman troops occupied territory there on a permanent basis. Yet the fact that Britons long remained defiant did not detract from Caesar's reputation. The sheer audacity of his effort delighted the Roman people, who saw it as the opening of another chapter in their great history of expansion and conquest. His first expedition to Britain won him 20 days of public thanksgiving in Rome, longer than for any of his other campaigns.

The hunger for such acclaim—and for wealth, slaves, and other prizes of war—did more to motivate Caesar and other venturesome commanders than their concern for the greater good of Rome. To be sure, Roman generals liked to portray their campaigns as necessary and their enemies as deserving of punishment. Caesar, for example, justified his attack on the Britons by claiming that they had aided the defiant Gauls. At heart, though, his expedition was a bravura performance by a general with his eyes firmly fixed on public opinion. To strengthen his position back home, he needed fresh military exploits abroad.

The dreams of ambitious noblemen like Caesar may have fueled the growth of the empire, but it was common soldiers and their everyday determination that secured victories and kept the vast Roman world intact. Like the generals, the soldiers had much to gain by campaigning hard, including a share in the spoils of conquest and a chance at promotion. But those rewards could not always be counted on, and other things besides self-interest kept the men marching and fighting—devotion to their fellow soldiers, loyalty to their commanders, and the conviction that it was better to die a free Roman in battle than to live as a slave of the enemy or return home defeated and disgraced.

Rome began its triumphant march from city-state to world power hundreds of years before the time of Caesar. And for most of that period, the Republic made do without professional soldiers. As late as the second century BC, Rome had no standing army. Instead, troops were drawn periodically from the population of male, property-owning citizens between the ages of 17 and 46. Those eligible for service were summoned to Rome, where they gathered by the thousands on the Capitoline Hill under the watchful eyes of the legions' principal officers.

The men were ranked by age and height, and to ensure that no one legion monopolized the prime candidates, officers from the various legions took their pick in turn. When more than

At left, legionaries construct a fort with squared chunks of turf in a detail from Trajan's Column, a monument celebrating one of Trajan's conquests and offering some of the finest illustrations of the Roman army at work. Such earthen forts were built hurriedly by soldiers to solidify their gains. To establish a permanent frontier, Romans built forts of wood or stone, interspersed with watchtowers like the one above, reconstructed in Germany.

enough candidates reported for the draft, those who were older or less fit were passed over. Romans considered military service a privilege, even though soldiers received only a small allowance and had to provide their own weapons and equipment.

This levy system worked well enough so long as most tours of duty were fairly brief, allowing recruits to return soon to their fields and families. But as Roman armies ventured ever farther afield to subdue foreign powers and guard distant frontiers, it became more difficult for busy citizen soldiers to look after their property or to have a career. Men campaigned for up to six years at a stretch and had to serve for a total of up to 16 years. Toward the end of the second century BC, widespread resentment toward the levy and the pressing need for more troops led the Roman consul Gaius Marius to overlook the property requirement for service and to entice poor citizens into the ranks by giving them arms and equipment at state expense. Many landless Romans who were scrounging for work in the cities flocked to enlist for terms of 16 years.

In time the new professional soldiers wanted better pay and retirement bonuses, and the task of providing those benefits fell to ambitious Roman generals, who often used their grateful troops as they saw fit. The soldiers commanded by Julius Caesar, for example, were fiercely loyal to him, and he retained their devotion in part by rewarding them with war booty and with bonuses from his own purse. Not long after doubling their pay, he led troops across the Rubicon and ousted his rival Pompey from Rome in 49 BC, before pursuing him to Greece and defeating him at Pharsalus a year later. Caesar's coup confirmed for anyone who still doubted it that supreme power was to be secured at sword point. That lesson was not lost on his grandnephew and adopted heir, Octavian, who later waged and won a civil war of his own against Mark Antony and his paramour, Cleopatra, and emerged as Augustus Caesar, Rome's first emperor.

Among the most pressing tasks of Augustus was to reduce to manageable size the huge Roman army, swollen by civil war. He cut the number of legions from about 60 to 28 and appeased the soldiers who were let go with money and land; some of the veterans founded new Roman settlements, both in Italy and around the empire. The remaining legions helped protect the empire and solidify its boundaries. Augustus completed the conquest of Spain and advanced the frontier in other places, but his goal was a secure empire with stable borders. And he came close to achieving that, although later emperors would add provinces by conquest until the empire reached its peak during the reign of Trajan in the early second century AD *(see map, pages 12-13)*. Under Augustus, legions became fixtures in the lands they held, with permanent camps that had barracks in place of tents.

Troops who spent most of their time defending frontiers could hope for little in the way of plunder, so Augustus did his best to secure their loyalty by promising legionaries a substantial bonus for completing their term of service, which he first set at 16 years and later extended to 20 years, followed by at least five years on reserve. Upon retirement a legionary would receive a lump-

der the command of a legate, appointed by the emperor. Few legates held their posts for more than three or four years, which lessened the chance that troops would become overly devoted to them and seasoned the commanders for more important jobs. Those who served well might become governors of provinces.

Each legate was assisted by six tribunes, the highest ranking of which was a young noble getting a taste of army life. The chief tribune's lack of military experience was compensated for by the camp prefect, typically an older man who had come up through the ranks and could be trusted to run the camp with a firm hand and

"Bludgeoning to death is the punishment for anyone who steals anything from the camp or who gives false evidence."

sum bonus equivalent to more than 13 years' salary, payable either in coin or in land of comparable value. Such measures were expensive, and Augustus paid for them in part with funds from his own purse, swelled by the wealth of Egypt, which he had claimed as his personal province after subduing Antony and Cleopatra. Like the good politician he was, Augustus made sure that the troops were well aware of his generosity.

The legionaries received higher pay than the army's many auxiliaries—noncitizens from the provinces, organized into units of up to 1,000 men under the command of a Roman officer. To retain their loyalty, Augustus's successors granted Roman citizenship to auxiliaries with 25 years of service as well as to their immediate family, enabling their sons to enlist as legionaries.

Augustus kept a tight rein on the army's commanders, the source of so much civil strife recently. Each legion was placed un-

assume command in the absence of the legate and chief tribune.

There was much experience too among the centurions—typically gruff, battle-hardened line officers who supervised the men closely, barking out orders and wielding vine swagger sticks to enforce discipline. In charge of units known as centuries—so called because they were meant to contain groups of 100 men, though the actual number varied—centurions had their own hierarchy. Each of the legion's 10 cohorts had a senior centurion, for example, and the senior centurion of the first cohort held the honored title of *primus pilus,* or first javelin, and had wide responsibilities.

Aside from the regular troops, each legion had a contingent of 120 cavalrymen, used chiefly as scouts, escorts, or messengers. (The army's fighting cavalrymen were auxiliaries from provinces renowned for their horsemanship.) There also were a number of men with specialized skills, such as engineers, surveyors, and car-

A horseman tramples his foe in this scene on the gravestone of Rufus Sita, a Thracian who served with the Romans in Britain as an auxiliary cavalryman in the first century AD. Cavalrymen earned more than infantrymen but less than legionaries.

penters who helped in the building of camps, bridges, roads and other projects that absorbed the legionaries when they were not waging war. Swelling the roster were armorers, physicians, and even musicians—one unit in Africa had 39 trumpeters and 36 horn players to rouse the men for action.

For the most part, legionaries were dedicated professionals. Would-be soldiers were closely scrutinized before they were accepted. They had to be dependable citizens, with no serious criminal offenses. Most were young men between the minimum age of 17 and 23, certified as fit by recruiters, who looked for candidates with keen eyes, broad chests, muscular shoulders, strong arms, and slim waists—high standards that were not always adhered to in practice. Similarly, recruiters for the prestigious first cohorts tried to find men who were at least five feet eight inches tall, but not many Romans of the day met that ideal.

Once a recruit swore an oath of loyalty to the emperor, he was admitted to the ranks and given a small sum to cover traveling expenses to his unit. There he embarked on a rigorous course of training. Three times a month he went on marches of nearly 20 miles, which had to be completed in about five hours. On campaign, each soldier carried not just his armor and weapons but also such essential supplies as a saw, pickax, sickle, basket, bucket, and rations—much of it bundled on a pole over the shoulder. Thus equipped, troops were less dependent on cumbersome and vulnerable baggage trains, a reform introduced earlier by the consul Marius and one that earned his soldiers the nickname "Marius's mules."

Novices also trained arduously for combat, wielding wicker shields and wooden swords and

RVFVS·SITA·EQVES·CHO·VI
TRACVM·ANN·XL·STIP·XXII
HEREDES·EXS·TEST·F·CVRAVE·S

assailing man-sized wooden stakes. Practice swords, shields, and javelins were all heavier than the genuine articles, so that real weapons seemed light to handle. Other training tasks included cutting down trees, jumping ditches, and swimming across rivers.

Discipline was harsh for novices and veterans alike. In this respect, conditions were likely much the same for soldiers during the reign of Augustus as for Roman troops two centuries earlier, when the Greek author Polybius noted that "bludgeoning to death is the punishment for anyone who steals anything from the camp or who gives false evidence." Another mortal transgression was falling asleep on watch. Those caught napping were condemned to be beaten or stoned by the men whose lives they had endangered, a punishment that could be deadly.

However strict, the military regimen was supremely effective. What carried Roman soldiers to victory was not so much superior weapons as superior training and discipline—the remarkable order they maintained in camp, on the road, and in battle.

Only seldom did that order collapse. Men sometimes found it hard to keep up their morale when faced with the prospect of spending the better part of their lives in strange and hostile country, without the compensations of regular family life. Although the principal officers might have their wives with them in camp, legionaries were not allowed to marry—a rule that remained in effect from the time of Augustus until nearly AD 200. Some soldiers formed lasting alliances with local women and had children by them, but such unions had no legal status. Even legionaries with unofficial families close by sometimes chafed at the restraints of army life. Men grew old and gray in the ranks, still subject to scoldings and beatings and wondering if they would ever have the chance to enjoy the retirement bonuses promised them. On rare occasions such smoldering resentments erupted into outright mutiny.

For all the efforts of Augustus to improve the army and fortify the empire, his death in AD 14 triggered major uprisings among legions stationed in Europe along the Danube and the Rhine. The mutineers hoped to pressure his successor, Tiberius, into shortening the 20-year term of service and abol-

Senior Roman officers and their wives, like this couple portrayed together on their grave in France, usually had their own houses at permanent army camps. Centurions and common soldiers, by contrast, could not legally marry, and any women involved with them lived off base.

ishing the reserve system that kept veterans on call for another five years or more in case of emergencies. Just such an emergency had arisen in AD 9—a devastating attack by German tribesmen that annihilated three legions and left the army so depleted along the northern frontier that many grizzled veterans ripe for retirement had to stay on. Stoking the fires of rebellion were the usual complaints about cruel or corrupt officers.

The revolt began along the Danube in the recently annexed province of Pannonia, where three legions were encamped. According to the Roman historian Tacitus, a firm believer in strict military discipline, part of the blame for the soldiers' uprising lay with their lax commander, Quintus Junius Blaesus, who, after learning of Augustus's death, allowed the men a rest from military duties. "This was the beginning of demoralization among the troops," wrote Tacitus, "of quarreling, of listening to the talk of every pestilent fellow, in short, of craving for luxury and idleness and loathing discipline and toil."

The chief agitator in the ranks, Tacitus noted, was a soldier named Percennius, who had learned how to incite a crowd by frequenting the theater as a paid applause leader. Percennius harangued dissatisfied troops, playing artfully to their resentments. Why should they obey like slaves, he asked them, and submit meekly to the demands of a few centurions and tribunes? Why should they endure dozens of campaigns and grow old and scarred, and still be asked to remain on reserve? Would there be no end of "floggings and wounds, of hard winters, wearisome summers, of terrible war, or barren peace"? Even those who survived the ordeal and reached retirement, Percennius said, were being offered land grants in place of cash that amounted to nothing more than marshy swamp or barren mountainside. He urged the soldiers to demand immediate relief in the form of a hefty pay hike, restoration of the 16-year term of service, an end to reserve duty, and prompt payment in hard cash of the bonus due on retirement.

Blaesus countered by addressing the troops himself and advising them to present their demands in the form of a request to the new emperor, Tiberius. The commander even agreed to send his own son, who was serving as one of his tribunes, to speak for them in Rome. Although this proposal was accepted by acclamation, it may have done more harm than good, persuading the soldiers, as Tacitus put it, that they could win "by compulsion what they had failed to obtain by good behavior."

The camp remained quiet for a while, but when other soldiers from the same legions who were out building roads and bridges learned of the protests, they went on a rampage, plundering the town of Nauportus and neighboring villages and attacking the officers who tried to restrain them. They pulled the camp prefect from his wagon, loaded him down with gear, and forced him to walk at the head of a column of jeering soldiers, who asked him how he liked having to bear heavy burdens for miles on end. (In fact,

Germanicus, nephew and adopted son of the emperor Tiberius, was described by Tacitus as a man of "unaspiring temper," unlike Tiberius, yet staunchly loyal to him. Germanicus spurned a proposal by his German legions in AD 14 that he lead them in revolt against Tiberius.

Toting their gear on poles, legionaries follow their standard-bearer across a bridge supported by boats in a relief from Trajan's Column. Along with their weapons, men on the march carried about 60 pounds of equipment. This type of hard labor contributed to the mutinies of AD 14, when older men on reserve duty in Germany begged Germanicus to free them from "such harassing service."

the prefect had once been a common soldier himself and had toiled as hard as anyone.)

The soldiers who had plundered Nauportus eventually returned to camp and stirred up fresh trouble. Men ransacked nearby settlements, and their commander responded by ordering centurions to arrest, whip, and imprison the more conspicuous looters as a lesson to the rest. When the detained men raised cries for help, their fellow soldiers stormed the guardhouse and set them free. Overrunning the camp, the mutineers forced most of the officers to flee and killed a centurion called Lucilius, a vicious disciplinarian who had earned the nickname "Bring Another," Tacitus related, "because when he had broken one vine-stick on a man's back, he would call in a loud voice for another and another."

Alarmed by the revolt, Tiberius sent his son Drusus and a detachment of the emperor's own Praetorian Guards to restore order. At first Drusus tried to placate the rebels, but he was met with defiance. Then fate came to his aid. An eclipse of the moon darkened the night sky, and the soldiers concluded that the gods were displeased with their behavior and had dimmed the heavens to warn them. Drusus seized the opportunity to work on the men's fears and induced most of them to return to their duties. Then he targeted the leaders of the mutiny. Percennius was among the first to be seized and executed, and others met the same fate after their fellow soldiers turned them in.

Meanwhile other legions had mutinied in Germany, where the troops nursed similar grievances and hoped to persuade their commander, Germanicus, to lead them in revolt against his uncle, Tiberius. Shortly after the uprising began, an unruly mob of soldiers gathered around Germanicus in camp and tried to win him over. According to Tacitus, some men grasped the commander's hand and "thrust his fingers into their mouths, that he might touch their toothless gums; others showed him their limbs bowed with age." Germanicus listened patiently to their complaints, but when men urged him to seize power with their help, he recoiled. Protesting that he "would die rather than cast off his loyalty," he raised his sword and threatened to kill himself if the mutineers did not let him go. An embittered soldier egged him on by offering him his own sword, saying it was sharper. But most of the troops were unwilling to see their commander come to grief, and they allowed him to return to his quarters.

Fearing that the rebellion would spread if he failed to make concessions, Germanicus endorsed the soldiers' demands, including the release from reserve duty of all those with more than 20 years' service. But when envoys from the Senate arrived at the camp, the soldiers feared that the promises made to them under duress would be revoked—as in fact they were—and renewed their threats. They accosted and nearly killed the chief envoy, who survived only by seeking sanctuary with the standard-bearer of the 1st Legion under the eagle. Tensions ran so high that Germanicus worried for the lives of his family if they remained with him in camp. Over the objections of his wife and cousin, Agrip-

This splendid gold-and-silver scabbard, with a portrait of the emperor Tiberius at its center, belonged to a senior Roman officer, who most likely received it from Tiberius as a gift.

pina the Elder, who protested that she was a "descendant of the Divine Augustus" and could face peril without flinching, he ordered her to leave with their young son, Caligula.

The tearful departure of the pregnant Agrippina and little Caligula, a favorite in camp, shamed the troops. Exploiting their remorse, Germanicus berated the men and challenged them to atone for their sins. Eager to escape punishment themselves, troops rounded up the ringleaders of the revolt and hacked them to death. "The soldiers gloated over the bloodshed," wrote Tacitus, "as though it gave them absolution."

Future emperors largely avoided such unrest by ensuring the army's loyalty: One of their first acts on coming to power was to pay a bonus to the troops. When legionaries did rise up in later years, it was usually to support the claim of their commander to supreme power. More often soldiers upheld the authority of the reigning emperor by beating back challenges from his enemies or rebellions by subject peoples. One such revolt flared up in the province of Judea in AD 66, and by the time it ended several years later, Roman troops and their fearsome siege machines had smashed through the walls of Jerusalem and reduced the holy city to rubble.

Witness to the siege was one Joseph ben Matthias, better known by his Roman name of Josephus. Born about AD 37 to an aristocratic family, he grew up in an atmosphere of crisis and controversy in Judea, which had come under Roman rule in recent times. Many there longed for independence. Some hoped for a messiah, an anointed one descended from the house of David and sent by God to deliver the

ROMANIZING THE PROVINCES

Gaul is crowded with traders and packed with Roman citizens," wrote Cicero in the first century BC. "No one in Gaul ever does business without the involvement of a Roman citizen." Cicero was referring to the Romans who flocked to Gaul and other occupied territories from Italy to run those provinces, but over the years many

provincials absorbed Roman culture, language, and law and became citizens themselves. The Romans won them over in part by building smaller versions of Rome throughout the empire, complete with temples, arenas, theaters, public baths, and forums. A number of those towns, like Cologne in Germany, were brand new. Others, like the old Gaulish village of Nîmes in present-day France, were greatly enlarged and enhanced with Roman monuments such as the Pont du Gard *(below)*, a bridge built in the early first century AD to carry an aqueduct to the town. A dependable water supply helped Nîmes grow into a vibrant administrative and trading center, and many who ventured there from surrounding areas felt the attraction of the Roman way of life.

A similar process was repeated in Roman provinces all around the Mediterranean and helped bring a long era of relative peace—the so-called Pax Romana—to an empire forged through conquest and coercion. Most Roman administrators were practical and tolerated native tradi-

Reminiscent of the murals at Pompeii and other Italian cities, this wall painting depicting Bacchus, the Roman god of wine *(above)*, adorned a home in Cologne, Germany, a town founded along the Rhine River as a Roman colony in the first century AD.

The arches of the Pont du Gard span the Gardon River near Nîmes, France. Water ran through a conduit at top, more than 160 feet above the river.

tions as long as they did not interfere with imperial prerogatives such as the collection of taxes or the observance of state rituals. People in rural areas largely adhered to their local customs, but those drawn to the cities soon learned to do as the Romans did. "They who lately disdained the tongue of Rome now coveted its eloquence," wrote Tacitus of the Celts in Roman Britain in the early second century AD. "Hence, too, a liking sprang up for our style of dress, and the 'toga' became fashionable." So deep and enduring was the Roman impact on the provinces that many beautiful works of classical design survive today across a vast area as reminders of a time when Rome offered its majesty to the world.

A columned facade provides a grand backdrop for this theater of Roman design in the Syrian city of Palmyra, a trading center linked by caravan to the Persian Gulf and India.

The arched entryway to the forum in the Tunisian city of Dougga frames a temple dedicated to the three chief Roman state gods: Jupiter, Juno, and Minerva.

An infant Bacchus rides a tiger in this elegant floor mosaic at El Djem in North Africa.

people from their oppressors, as prophesied in scripture. One small messianic group whose faith would ultimately transform the Roman world said that the savior had recently appeared—a man named Jesus, born in the Judean town of Bethlehem during the reign of Augustus and later crucified by Roman troops in Jerusalem, only to rise from the grave, according to his disciples. Jesus had counseled hard-pressed Roman subjects to offer Caesar that which belonged to him—the coins that bore his image and were due to him as taxes—while reserving for God the higher tribute of their prayers and devotion.

An increasing number of Judeans in Josephus's time resented the idea of rendering any kind of tribute to Caesar. Josephus charged that Roman governors of the province, not content with levying steep taxes, extorted bribes from the populace. He wrote that Gessius Florus, who governed Judea from AD 64 to 66, "virtually announced to the entire country that everyone might be a bandit if he chose, so long as he himself received a rake-off." Some of those "bandits" were actually rebels, agitating for independence. They found a receptive audience among devout Judeans who abhorred the cult of the divine emperor and hated to see the Roman eagle paraded about Jerusalem like a heathen idol. Adding to their outrage was the presence in Judea of foreign auxiliaries who had little sympathy for the local people and often clashed with them.

Josephus, for his part, disdained the idea of rebelling against Rome. A priest and a member of the Pharisee sect—noted for its strict adherence to Jewish law and ritual—he believed that the Roman occupation was ordained by God. Furthermore, experience taught him that there was more to be gained by cooperating with the Romans than by defying them. While still in his twenties, he sailed with others to Rome to secure the release of some fellow priests sent to answer charges before the emperor Nero. In Italy Josephus encountered a Judean actor who introduced him to Nero's wife Poppaea, and with her help he succeeded in his mission. He came away with an increased regard for the Romans.

Josephus returned to his homeland in AD 66 to find the province on the verge of revolt. Gessius Florus had confiscated money from the treasury of the temple in Jerusalem "on the pretext that Caesar required it," as Josephus put it. A riot ensued that was put down by troops at terrible cost, further inciting the extreme opponents of Roman rule. Militant Judeans took up arms and seized control of Jerusalem. The revolt spread, and moderates like Josephus, who could no longer hope for reconciliation with Rome, joined the war effort. He was appointed military commander of Galilee, the northernmost district of Judea. That put him directly in the path of the Roman commander and future emperor Vespasian, who would soon bear down on the rebels from Syria with three legions.

Josephus had little hope of prevailing against the well-trained Romans. "Every day," he wrote later of the Roman army regimen, "each soldier exercises with as much intensity as he would in war. This is the reason why the shock of war affects them so little. No confusion ruins their customary neat formations, nor are they paralysed by fear, or worn out with fatigue. Victory over enemies who have experienced none of this comes sure and certain. One would not be wrong in saying that their maneuvers are like bloodless battles, and their battles bloodstained maneuvers."

When Vespasian and his legions marched into Galilee in AD 67, most of the troops mustered by Josephus fled in disarray. Those who remained under his command retreated with him to the citadel at Jotapata, where they came under siege for more than six weeks. After scaling the walls, the Romans swept

A bearded prisoner and his forlorn wife *(left, from a Roman sarcophagus)* and defeated fighting men fleeing a town being put to the torch *(above, from Trajan's Column)* exemplify the plight of people conquered by Roman soldiers. Romans sometimes spared the populace of hostile regions if they yielded readily, but groups like the defiant Judeans were treated ruthlessly and killed or enslaved in droves.

through the streets, killing those in their path. Josephus and a few dozen others were hiding out in a cave, where he urged his companions to accept the defeat as God's will and appeal to Vespasian for mercy. The others rejected his advice, and Josephus joined them in a suicide pact. After all but one of his companions had died, however, he persuaded his fellow survivor to surrender with him to the Romans.

Taken before Vespasian, Josephus won his captor's favor by prophesying that the Roman commander would one day become emperor—a prediction fulfilled in 69 AD, when Vespasian emerged triumphant from the bloody civil wars that followed Nero's suicide a year earlier. Before returning to Rome, Vespasian delegated to his son Titus the task of capturing Jerusalem and ending the rebellion. Josephus accompanied Titus and chronicled the siege that followed.

When Titus reached Jerusalem with four legions and numerous supporting troops in AD 70, he confronted one of the most impressive strongholds Roman troops had ever come up against. His men would have to break through several walls, including one encircling the newer part of town that had grown up north of the older core of Jerusalem, another protecting the markets in the middle of town, and a stout barrier replete with towers and battlements shielding the temple. Built on the site of the original Temple of King Solomon, this splendid hilltop structure was encased in white stone and adorned with gold. From a distance, Josephus marveled, it gleamed "like a mountain covered with snow."

A strong and united Jerusalem might have better withstood Titus's assault. But the population was sharply divided, Josephus reported, with militant factions vying with one another for supremacy and attacking those who advocated surrender. Furthermore, Jerusalem was prey to famine once the Romans severed its supply routes.

In preparation for the assault, the Romans built imposing siege towers—75-foot-high platforms sheathed in iron plates to prevent the foe from setting fire to the wood-

Below, Roman soldiers depicted on Trajan's Column advance under cover of their shields in the formation called the testudo—a tactic used in conjunction with battering rams like the model above to reduce Judean strongholds.

en framework. Ascending these towers for battle, Titus's forces loomed over the Judeans defending the outer wall and pelted them with javelins, arrows, and stones. Meanwhile other Roman troops began pounding the wall with a massive battering ram. Josephus described a similar Roman ram used at Jotapata, which consisted of a huge log tipped with iron in the shape of a ram's head and suspended from supporting beams by ropes that allowed the soldiers to swing the log back and forth, driving it home repeatedly with shattering effect.

On the 15th day of the siege, the outer wall was breached, but Titus's advancing troops made only fitful progress in the days ahead as the city's defenders put up fierce resistance. After lengthy fighting that surged back and forth, the Romans broke down a stretch of the second wall and occupied the market area, advancing past

the Romans, he claimed, but others reviled him and held fast.

When surrender was not forthcoming, Titus prepared to renew the assault. The struggle that ensued lasted for weeks and began with an attack on the Antonia Fortress, which towered above one corner of the temple precinct and was crucial to its defense. Roman troops standing atop newly erected siege towers bombarded the defenders there, while rams pounded the fortress wall and men dug away at its foundation under the cover of shields raised overhead by soldiers in a tight formation known as a testudo, or tortoise. Even after breaching the barrier and capturing the fortress, the Romans had to fight furiously for many days to reach the gates of the temple, where rebel leaders were ensconced with their followers. Finally, more than three months after the siege commenced, soldiers entered the sanctuary and set it afire.

"*They poured into the streets sword in hand, cut down without mercy all who came within reach.*"

shops and stalls toward the great rampart protecting the temple.

Before assailing that barrier, Titus tried to prod the defenders into surrendering. He staged a splendid parade of his troops on their payday in order to prove to the onlooking Judeans that their enemies were equipped to keep up the fight as long as necessary. And he sent Josephus to harangue the defenders in their own language for persisting in a hopeless cause and imperiling their city and loved ones. "Turn round and gaze at the beauty of what you are betraying," Josephus urged them. "If the sight of these things leaves you unmoved, at least pity your families, and let each man set before his eyes his wife and children and parents, so soon to perish by famine or the sword." Some of his starving listeners were moved by his appeals and deserted to

After the temple crumbled, troops besieged the populace in the older part of town and laid waste to the district. "They poured into the streets sword in hand," Josephus wrote of the conquering soldiers, "cut down without mercy all who came within reach, and burnt the houses of any who took refuge indoors, occupants and all."

Many of the survivors were deported as slaves or subjected to other forms of punishment. Hundreds were dispatched to Rome and paraded through the streets there in the triumph that Titus celebrated with Vespasian. Dressed as conquerors in crimson robes and wreathed in laurel, the emperor and his son sat on a dais in ivory chairs while their soldiers shouted acclamations.

Once the triumphal procession began, Romans thronged the

streets to gaze in awe at huge traveling stages, depicting the war in vivid tableaux. "Here was to be seen a smiling countryside laid waste," Josephus related, "there whole formations of the enemy put to the sword; men in flight and men led off to captivity; walls of enormous size thrown down by engines, great strongholds stormed." Displayed in the procession were spoils of war wrested from the temple, including the golden seven-branched menorah, or candelabrum, and a scroll described by Josephus as the Jewish law, perhaps the Torah, which included the divine commandments handed down to Moses. For the sorrowful captives who trudged through the streets, there could be no greater loss than this—to surrender to Caesar treasures from the house of God.

Major challenges to Roman authority such as the revolt in Judea were infrequent in the decades that followed. When not expanding frontiers for venturesome emperors like Trajan, soldiers devoted much of their time to peaceful tasks. They built bridges with graceful arches that would stand for ages, and high-

ways that proved equally durable and facilitated trade as well as troop movements. Although legionaries grumbled about such work, they took pride in their proficiency. One soldier wrote scathingly of civilians who were assigned to bore holes for an aqueduct into opposite sides of a hill—and dug past each other without meeting. "If you want a decent job," he advised, "get the army to do it."

Over the years, the complexion of the legions changed. By AD 100, only about one legionary in five was Roman born. The overwhelming majority of new recruits were men from the provinces, including the sons of auxiliaries who had been awarded citizenship for their service. Many of the foreign-born legionaries already knew some Latin when they enlisted; others picked up enough of the language to follow orders. Recruits without Roman names adopted them, like the young Egyptian called Apion, who casually informed his parents in writing after enlisting with the Romans that his name was now Antonius Maximus.

The flood of provincials into the ranks did not bring an end to the tensions between soldiers and local people, in part because recruits from one province often served in another. Even soldiers on their home ground sometimes antagonized the civilians. One common grievance against the troops was their habit of requisitioning pack animals when on the march. The Greek philosopher Epictetus, born about AD 55, had suitably Stoic advice to offer on the subject: "If a requisition is taking place and a soldier takes your mule, let it go, do not hold onto it, and do not complain. For if you do, you will get a beating and lose your mule just the same."

Despite frictions, the presence of troops with ties to the surrounding communities often helped reconcile restive provinces to Roman rule. Even Britain, where Julius Caesar and his men had encountered such fierce opposition, eventually became a dependable outpost of the empire, where legionaries mingled with the locals and many young Britons volunteered to serve under Roman authority. Such accord did not come easily. It took four legions under the emperor Claudius to secure southernmost Britain in AD 43, and resistance was strong for a long time to come. Soldiers clashed with hostile Britons from the lowlands of East Anglia to the mountains of Wales. By late in the century, Roman troops had advanced all the way to the Scottish Highlands, but the task of subduing that region proved too much, and the Romans withdrew to a line about 20 miles south of the present border between England and Scotland. The frontier was established along a military road known as the Stanegate, reinforced with timber forts and

Romans celebrate their triumph over the Judeans by carrying the menorah and other spoils from the temple in Jerusalem through the streets of Rome in this detail from the Arch of Titus, built to commemorate his victory. The coin above, minted in AD 70, shows a proud Roman soldier beside a grief-stricken woman representing Iudaea Capta, or Captive Judea.

watchtowers. Then in AD 122 the emperor Hadrian bolstered the line by beginning construction of the 73-mile-long stone bulwark that became known as Hadrian's Wall.

At first life on this far frontier must have been lonely for the soldiers garrisoning it. The nearest legionary bases were at Chester and York, several days' march to the south. Early on, the troops at the border posts were auxiliaries from other provinces such as Spain and Gaul, commanded by Roman officers. They may well have found this hinterland strange and desolate, but their life was not without compensations, as evidenced by documents found at the site of a fort called Vindolanda, one of the bigger posts along the Stanegate line.

Penned in ink, mostly on thin wooden tablets, between about AD 90 and the time Hadrian's Wall was being built, these revealing documents include daily accounts and duty rosters as well as letters from home, delivered to the soldiers along with gifts. The accounts show that the troops enjoyed a varied diet, including Celtic beer, imported wine, wheat, ham, and venison. And the presents from home added to their comforts: One letter lists the contents of a gift parcel, including sandals, socks, and two pairs of underwear. The socks—something Roman soldiers in warmer climates did without—

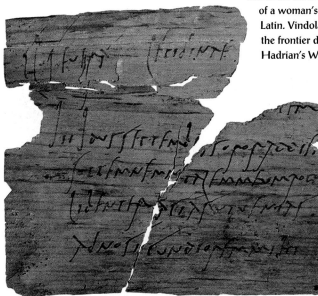

Penned on wood about AD 100 and found at the site of Vindolanda, a Roman fort in Britain, this birthday invitation to an officer's wife, Sulpicia Lepidina, from her friend Claudia Severa marks the earliest surviving example of a woman's handwriting in Latin. Vindolanda lay along the frontier defined later by Hadrian's Wall *(right).*

must have been greatly appreciated here in northern Britain.

Another letter offers a rare glimpse of conditions for officers' wives, who lived surrounded by men and plainly cherished the opportunity to visit with female friends or relatives. The letter was sent around the year AD 100 to Sulpicia Lepidina, the wife of a commander of a unit at Vindolanda, by a friend who addressed her affectionately as sister, Claudia Severa. Severa's husband probably served as an officer at another northern fort. "I cordially invite you, sister, to make sure that you come to us on 11 September for the day of the celebration of my birthday," wrote Claudia Severa, who added fondly that "you will make the day more pleasant for me by your arrival." She offered her best wishes to her friend's husband as well and passed along greetings

been stabbed to death were found buried beneath the floorboards.

Overall, soldiers on the British frontier enjoyed considerable freedom, extending to matters of worship. Although the army sponsored patriotic festivals devoted to the traditional Roman gods and the divine emperors, the men were allowed to honor their favorite cults outside camp. Small temples dedicated to Mithras, a god of Persian origin revered by soldiers in many parts of the empire, were located a short distance from Vindolanda. Other shrines in the area were dedicated to the Syrian goddess Astarte and the demigod Hercules. One commander in Britain, a native of North Africa, wrote a poem to the goddess Tanit, the Carthaginian version of Astarte. And soldiers on the frontier cast coins for good luck into a spring sacred to the local goddess Coventina.

"*You will make the day more pleasant for me by your arrival.*"

from her own husband and young son. The body of the letter was written out by a scribe, but she added an endearing postscript in her own hand: "I shall expect you, sister. Be well, sister, my dearest love, and so may I be."

Officers' wives were not the only women in the area; others resided near the posts in settlements that sprouted up to meet the soldiers' needs. Although auxiliaries, like legionaries, were prohibited from marrying, officers could not stop them from forming unions with local women, who set up house with the children as close to the men as possible. Nearby settlements were also home to prostitutes, merchants, and innkeepers, who afforded off-duty troops a place to drink and gamble. Some soldiers may also have vented frustrations in violent fashion—at one inn excavated near Hadrian's Wall, the remains of a man and a woman who had

Men at the posts found other outlets for their energies besides battle. One local commander boasted of his prowess in an inscription by claiming credit not for some conquest but for "the capture of a boar of exceptionally fine appearance," which his predecessors had tried and failed to snare. At Vindolanda, meanwhile, a tannery turned out footwear for men, women, and children—articles meant for the family members of the troops, perhaps, or for sale to others in the community.

Eventually, forts such as Vindolanda were garrisoned by local recruits, who commonly passed the job from father to son. Like other Romanized Britons, they had embraced the ways of the conquerors. But Rome had won them over not just by force of arms but by yielding power and privileges to people once spurned as barbarians.

THE SPIRIT OF THE GODS

"We Romans owe our supremacy over all other peoples," declared Cicero in the first century BC, "to our piety and religious observances and to our wisdom in believing that the spirit of the gods rules and directs everything." This belief in the power of the gods came from the earliest Romans, farmers who felt that spirits inhabited and controlled everything in nature.

Contact with foreigners broadened their established religious beliefs considerably. The Etruscans as well as the Greeks brought new gods and new rites to the Romans. Lacking their own mythology, the Romans eventually absorbed all 12 Greek Olympians into their pantheon. And as the empire expanded in succeeding centuries, Romans continued to assimilate deities from the lands they conquered.

The Roman god Hercules, adapted from Greek mythology, recognizes his son in a fresco from Herculaneum. Before incorporating Greek myths into their own beliefs, Romans did not portray the gods in their art.

125

WINNING THE FAVOR OF THE ANCIENT GODS

Roman religious observance included both domestic worship and official state ritual. Domestic worship meant gaining and keeping the goodwill of the gods presiding over one's home, family, and property. Devout families gathered daily at the household shrine, or lararium, offering incense, wine, or "sacred meal mingled with crackling salt" to their spirit guardians. The goddess Vesta ruled the hearth; the lares were protective ancestral household spirits. The pe-nates safeguarded the cupboard, and the genius was the spiritual essence of the family.

Official religion evolved from these domestic rites, but its aim was to ensure and preserve the prosperity of the state. The emperor served as head of the religion, and state officials functioned as priests. Citizens were to attend the ceremonies, standing in silence while a veiled priest recited the prayers. The rituals were so precise that any mistake or deviation caused the priest to begin all over again. Gifts—incense, wine, or animals—were then offered to the gods to ward off pestilence or disease, to gain victory in battle, or in thanksgiving.

The state also sanctioned monthly festivals (an outgrowth of early agricultural rites), with specific deities honored each month. Most popular was the Saturnalia, a seven-day celebration beginning on December 17, where gifts were exchanged and slaves were waited on by their masters.

At right, a farmer passes by an outdoor shrine. The table in the center is laden with fruit, an offering for a goddess whose small sanctuary is at top left.

A lararium painting features two lares dancing on either side of a household spirit, or genius. Below them is a serpent, symbol of fertility.

Sacrificial animals are led to the slaughter in a state religious ritual dedicated to the god Mars. The veiled celebrant at near left offers a libation at the altar.

SEEKERS OF SALVATION

Dissatisfied with the impersonal nature of the state religion, many Romans turned to foreign cults, which seemed to offer more personal involvement in their rituals as well as the promise of redemption and eternal life. At first the state tried to suppress interest in these cults, but they survived, and so it tolerated them as long as citizens also attended official ceremonies.

One of the first to find favor with the Romans was the cult of Cybele, the Asian nature goddess. Ceremonies centered on the annual death and rebirth of her consort, Attis, and worship was characterized by orgiastic dancing, sometimes ending in self-castration by her all-male priests. The cult of Isis, Egyptian goddess of fertility and marriage, embraced a sim-

The offerings above—a severed ox head, an overturned cup of blood, and fruit—and the initiation ritual at right probably represent a Roman adaptation of a Dionysian rite.

A high priest of the cult of Cybele holds a pine cone, symbol of Cybele's lover, Attis, in his left hand, and a flail, used in initiation ceremonies, in his right hand.

White-robed priests of Isis perform a water purification ritual as chanting devotees line the steps of the goddess's temple in this wall painting from Herculaneum.

"Whose is the realm, his is the religion."

Mithras plunges his dagger into the bull whose sacrificial blood was a symbol of life after death for the followers of this Persian god.

The outline of a dove with an olive branch, a Christian symbol of salvation, was scratched on the wall of an underground catacomb where followers hid during times of persecution.

ilar theme of resurrection and immortality.

Dionysus, Greek god of wine and youth, achieved widespread popularity in his original form or as the Romanized Bacchus. Frightened by stories of the drunken frenzies of its followers, the Roman Senate proscribed the cult's rites, known as the Bacchanalia, in 186 BC, but worship continued in secret. Mithras was a Persian god who personified truth and light, locked in an eternal struggle against the forces of darkness and evil. His rituals were restricted to men and appealed to soldiers of the Roman army.

The beliefs espoused by many of these cults—moral conduct on earth and eternal life after death—made the inroads of the cult of Christianity possible. Though persecuted on and off for centuries, Christianity became the official religion of the Roman Empire in the fourth century AD.

ANNIAE
ARESCVSA

CHAPTER FOUR

THE GLORY
OF THE GAMES

Reins wrapped securely around his waist, a charioteer lashes his horses toward the turning posts, where drivers sometimes lost control and crashed. Such suspenseful moments were common at Roman *ludi*, games where spectators reveled in the feats of charioteers and gladiators and the dramatic flights of actors.

omans had never witnessed a triumphal procession quite like this. Returning to Italy from Greece in AD 67, the emperor Nero landed at Naples and had part of the city wall torn down to signal his glorious feats. Then he made his way to Rome and entered the capital in the same chariot that had been used earlier by Augustus to celebrate victory. But Nero was no conventional conqueror. As indicated by the Olympic wreath around his brow, he had prevailed not in battle but in a host of athletic and artistic contests in Greece, where obliging judges had awarded him a phenomenal 1,808 prizes and confirmed his inflated opinion of himself as a great and versatile performer, master of stage, circus, and arena.

In truth the results said little about the virtue of his performances. At Olympia, for instance, he had competed in a chariot race driving a 10-horse team, a stunt he himself once derided. Most charioteers of the day drove four-horse teams, and even that demanded great strength and agility. Predictably, Nero's attempt ended in failure. After falling from his chariot and being helped back in, he quit the race before reaching the finish line. The judges deferred to his majesty and declared him the winner nonetheless.

The great Circus Maximus—portrayed at left on a second-century-AD coin and at far right in a model of Imperial Rome—could hold far more spectators for its races than could attend gladiatorial bouts at the Colosseum *(top center)* or performances at the Marcellus Theater *(bottom left)*.

Nero's victories may have been contrived, but his passion for performing was genuine. As a youngster, he had followed closely the exploits of the leading charioteers. Once, a teacher caught him neglecting his studies to tell fellow pupils of a driver who fell during a race and was caught in the reins and dragged along by his team. (Nero tried to lie his way out of trouble by claiming that he had actually been discussing the Trojan hero Hector, who was subjected to something similar in Homer's *Iliad*.) The young emperor was equally fascinated by the spellbinding gifts of actors and singers and sought to strengthen his voice for the stage by lying on his back with a heavy stone on his chest. He loved staging bizarre spectacles and once forced hundreds of men of high rank to fight each other in the arena.

Aristocratic Romans despised Nero for such displays and for condescending to compete in chariot races and perform on the stage himself—activities considered fit only for people of low origins. Common people, on the other hand, appreciated Nero's showmanship and readily celebrated his Olympian feats. Fittingly, the triumphal procession he staged after returning from Greece passed through the Circus Maximus—the vast racetrack in Rome where charioteers vied for glory—then continued on through the Forum. Nero was showered with ribbons and other tokens of esteem, and animals were sacrificed along the route to honor the occasion.

Afterward Nero draped his sleeping quarters with his victory wreaths and commissioned statues of himself singing and playing the lyre. During the months to come he grew increasingly concerned about straining his precious voice. "It never occurred to him that he ought to refrain from singing, or even sing a little less," Suetonius commented in his unsparing chronicle of Nero's reign. Instead, the emperor rested his voice by addressing his troops only in writing or through a spokesman, and he attended no official ceremonies without a voice trainer at his side to tell him "when to spare his vocal cords, and when to protect his mouth with a handkerchief."

It said much about Nero and his times that he considered military and administrative matters of less consequence than the pleasures of the stage or circus. His tendency to worry more about his artistic performances than about his role as supreme commander would soon come back to haunt him. Many Romans shared his passion for games, however, and the empire appeared none the worse for it, in part because the provinces were so productive. Grain from abroad nourished the capital, and foreign recruits ably defended distant frontiers, allowing Romans to devote a considerable amount of time to revelry. By Nero's reign, roughly 80 days a year were devoted to *ludi,* or games, including chariot races, blood sports, and theatrical shows. In addition, emperors proclaimed special celebrations to mark victories or other great events during their reigns. Not all business came to a halt

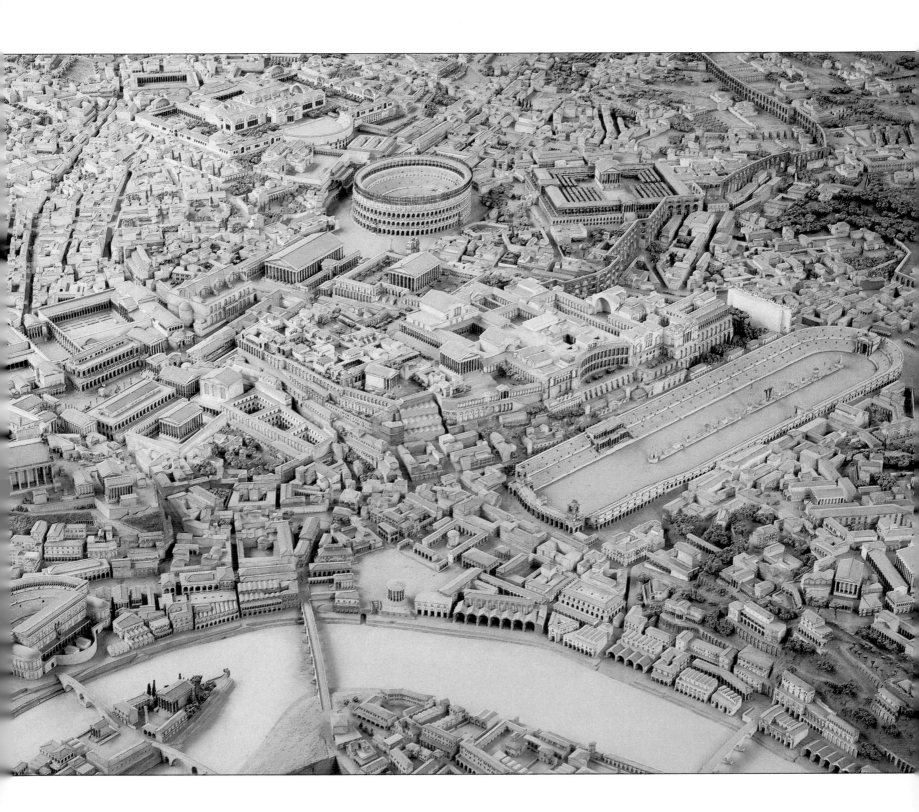

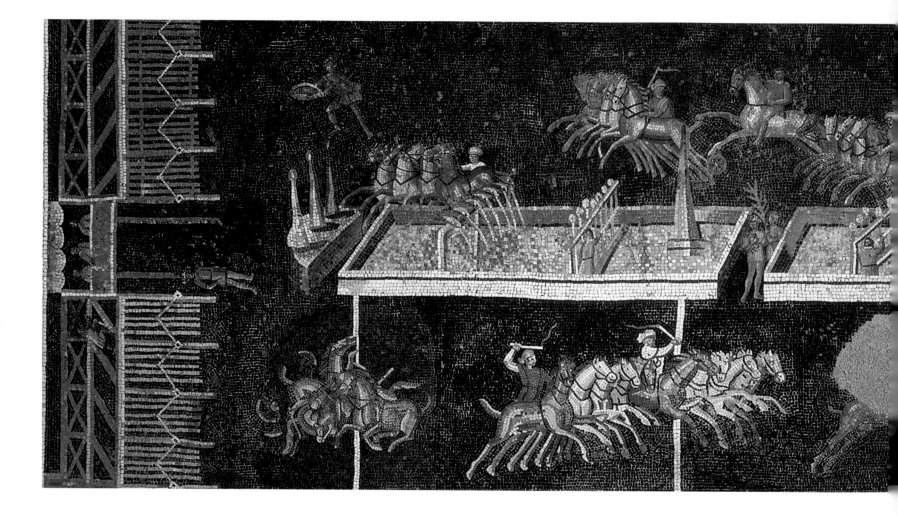

on these festive occasions, but for as long as the games lasted, the main task of Romans was to enjoy themselves.

Common people had further reason to cherish the games, because the gatherings brought them in touch with their leaders and made them feel privileged. Rulers who hoped to endear themselves to the masses had little choice but to stage lavish entertainments. Julius Caesar spent extravagantly on games to bolster his reputation, and Roman emperors in later times were no less generous in their outlays. The satirist Juvenal scoffed at the masses for their obsession with the "bread and circuses" doled out

to them. Yet the games were more than mere diversions. They were meant to honor the gods, and though they lost much of their spiritual significance over time, they remained important civic rituals, celebrating the strength and competitiveness that made Rome great.

Chariot racing was the oldest and most popular of the public entertainments. According to legend, Romulus organized a day of chariot racing soon after he founded Rome. The original Circus Maximus, located in a swampy valley between the Aventine and Palatine Hills, was reportedly laid out in the days of the

Etruscan kings. The great Circus Maximus of imperial times, however, was the work of Julius Caesar, who began the reconstruction, and of Augustus, who completed it. Later emperors added embellishments, including more seating and an increasingly elaborate facade, graced with shops and arcades.

There were other circuses in Rome and around the empire, but none surpassed the Circus Maximus. Measuring 680 yards long and 150 yards wide, it seated roughly 150,000 spectators—or three times as many as the Colosseum, the main amphitheater in imperial Rome for blood sports—and many more fans settled for standing room or watched from the hills overlooking the circus. To be assured of a seat, people began arriving before dawn. The lower tier was designated for senators and equestrians. Others were relegated to the upper tiers, where the seating was particularly cramped and uncomfortable (many spectators brought cushions). The crowded conditions had at least one advantage, however. Ovid, a poet celebrated for his love lyrics, noted approvingly that a suitor could hardly avoid touching his female companion as they sat side by side at the races and that he could win her gratitude by asking the man behind her "not to jab her in the back with his knees."

A day at the races began with a parade through the streets of Rome to the circus. Traditionally, the presiding magistrate led the way in his chariot, accompanied by attendants and followed by musicians. Then came the stars of the event, the charioteers themselves, carefully guiding their spirited horses through the narrow streets. Behind them trailed priests and incense bearers, along with the images of gods and goddesses, carried aloft on biers or in chariots.

The spectators might root for a particular charioteer, but they were mainly attached to the faction the driver and horses belonged to. There were four such factions in all—the Greens, Reds, Blues, and Whites—and each had its own racing colors, stables, trainers, grooms, and

Two wrecked vehicles lie at either end of the track as surviving drivers hurry on in this mosaic of a chariot race. Race officials turn lap markers and hold the victory wreath and palm branch *(center)* or throw water onto overheated wheels *(top left)*. The presiding magistrate at such races relished the honor of tossing the starting cloth and liked to be remembered in that pose *(right)*.

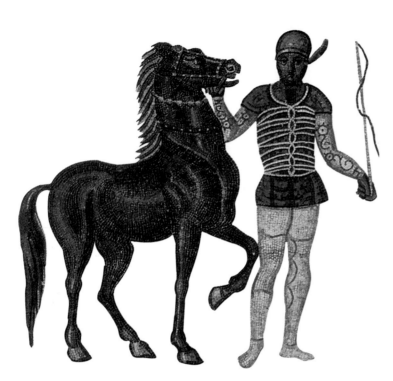

zealous fans. A foul by a member of one faction against another could spark a riot in the stands. Pliny the Younger, a prominent orator and public official, professed disdain for the frenzy of the spectators and gave thanks that "their pleasure is not mine," but he may have enjoyed the sport more than he let on. He wore a signet ring bearing the image of a chariot and team.

Fans had plenty to get worked up about, because drivers often tried to maneuver their opponents into crashes. Fallen drivers, having tied the reins around their waists to give them better control of the horses, might be dragged to their deaths if they could not cut themselves loose in time with the dagger they wore at their waist. One of the best accounts of the drama and danger of chariot racing was offered by the poet Sidonius Apollinaris, who wrote in the fifth century AD but described a contest that was not unlike those run at the circus in Nero's time.

Apollinaris told of a race in which his friend Consentius

competed, involving four four-horse teams that could be clearly identified in the starting gates by their colors: white, blue, green, and red. In the tense moments before the race, grooms tried to calm the nervous horses with soothing pats and soft words, but the animals still stamped and snorted. When the starter gave the signal, trumpets blared, and the four teams charged from the gates, raising clouds of dust. Consentius held his horses back for six laps and let the other drivers vie for the lead. Then as he made for the far turn in the seventh and final lap, he planted his feet firmly on the floorboard and urged his team on. One driver had already exhausted his horses and pulled out. A second felt Consentius closing in on him, tried to make too sharp a turn at the post, and spun out of control. The third driver took too wide a turn, allowing Consentius to pass him on the inside, then cut back sharply in an effort to catch up and fell to his death when his horses stumbled and his chariot overturned. Safely ahead, Consentius drove on alone to the finish line and received the coveted palm branch of victory.

Despite the hazards of the sport, some drivers enjoyed long and successful careers. Gilded busts of leading charioteers adorned public places, and rulers befriended the champions and lavished them with gifts. The emperor Caligula reportedly gave 20,000 gold pieces to a driver for the Greens, his favorite faction. Such tribute must have been dizzying for the charioteers, many of whom began their careers as slaves. Their regular earnings went to their owners, who typically rewarded the driver with a portion of the purse. In time a gifted charioteer might purchase his freedom and negotiate for better terms from the faction owners. To some Romans the sums paid to charioteers appeared excessive. Juvenal complained that a driver might earn 100 times more than a lawyer. But charioteers faced great risks, and many died before achieving freedom or fame.

Among the greatest drivers was a man of Spanish birth named Gaius Appuleius Diocles, whose remarkable career was detailed in an inscription in Rome. Diocles came there as a youth and began racing for the Whites in AD 122, when he was 18 years old. Such were the challenges of the sport that it took him two years to win his first race, but he was spectacularly successful thereafter, and his services were soon coveted by other factions. He switched to the Greens in AD 128 and moved to the Reds a few years later, remaining with them for the rest of his career. A great driver like Diocles

Clad in rigid leather helmets and chest protectors of interwoven leather strips, four charioteers sport the colors of their teams: Greens, Whites, Reds, and Blues. The emperor Nero was fiercely devoted to the Greens and wore a coat of that color at the track.

THE MAGNIFICENT COLOSSEUM

Adorned with white marble and gilded passageways, the Colosseum *(right)*—so called for the colossal statue of Nero that stood nearby—was an impressive and fearsome place, steeped in the blood of gladiators and wild beasts. Begun around AD 70 by the emperor Vespasian, the 50,000-seat arena was opened in AD 80 by his son and heir, Titus.

The complex was added on to by Titus's younger brother and successor, Domitian, credited with installing the underground cells for wild beasts *(below)*. When the show began, men hoisted the animals in open-ended cages from the lowest level to the next, where there were no front bars to hold them in. Desperate for freedom, the animals raced up ramps and exited through trapdoors into the arena—to kill or be killed.

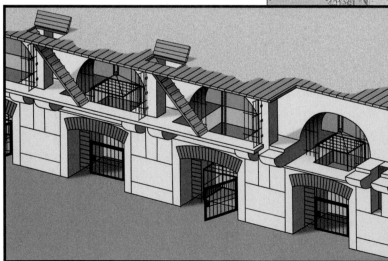

eventually achieved a kind of free agency and could choose which faction to race for.

By the time Diocles retired at the age of 42, after nearly a quarter-century in competition, he had won an astonishing 1,462 races of the 4,257 he entered—many of them involving two or three teams from each of the four factions. In more than half his victories, he led from start to finish, but when pressed, he out-dueled his competitors and won more than 500 races in the closing stretch. Like the great jockeys of later times, he had fine horses to work with, and drove one stalwart animal to victory 200 times. In an era when a Roman legionary earned about 1,200 sesterces a year, Diocles garnered 36 million sesterces in prize money over his career. Part of that went to the faction owners, but he still must have been enormously wealthy.

Diocles was a perfect role model for a society that worshiped victory. In the circus, as in battle or politics, Romans would do just about anything to gain an edge. Fans even cast spells on the rivals of their favorites. "I conjure you up, holy beings and holy names," read the inscription on one curse tablet; "join in aiding this spell, and bind, enchant, thwart, strike, overturn, conspire against, destroy, kill, break Eucherius, the charioteer, and all his horses tomorrow in the circus at Rome."

For all the perils faced by charioteers, men who did battle in the arena confronted even greater risks. About the best they could hope for was to match the feats of the gladiator Severus, a slave who won his freedom by fighting. What became of him is unknown, but a portrait in Pompeii showed him vanquishing a foe in his 55th bout—a long career for a man in his perilous trade.

From the beginning there was something sacrificial about the gladiators' role. Their contests, known as *munera,* or obligations, derived from Etruscan rites designed to honor dead heroes with displays of courage and bloodshed. The first documented ritual of this kind at a Roman funeral was held in 264 BC and

involved three pairs of gladiators, all of them slaves. Soon Roman families were staging bouts with many more contestants, both to honor the dead and gain prestige.

By early imperial times, the contests had lost their religious significance and become public entertainments, staged on their own or in conjunction with chariot races and other spectacles during festivals. The emperor sometimes served as the sponsor and host in Rome, and local dignitaries often played that role elsewhere. Bouts in the arena between gladiators were often supplemented by *venationes,* or wild-animal "hunts," pitting leopards, lions, elephants, crocodiles, and other imported beasts against one another or against humans, unarmed or armed (a separate class of fighters, the *bestiarii,* were trained and equipped to combat animals). At the grand opening of the Colosseum in AD 80, Titus sponsored 100 days of carnage involving more than 10,000 fighting men and hordes of animals, 9,000 of which perished.

Amphitheaters like the Colosseum were built especially for the staging of such bloodfests. Previously, the shows had been held in circuses, forums, or other public places, which proved dangerous for spectators. At one show, frightened elephants nearly stampeded into the crowd. To protect against mishaps, the lowest seats in the Colosseum were situated well above the killing ground, and the animals were kept securely caged before the events in underground cells, where they must have raised an infernal din.

Located near the Colosseum was one of the training schools where gladiators learned their craft. Severus probably trained at the school in Pompeii, considered one of the best. Like soldiers, trainees sparred with weapons that were heavier than those used in actual combat. The prospects of would-be gladiators might be bleak, but the owners kept the men strong and fit, providing them with good doctors. The great Greek physician Galen began his career treating gladiators in the mid-second century AD and later became the court doctor of the emperor Marcus Aurelius.

Severus fought in the Pompeii Amphitheater, the oldest surviving structure of its kind, completed around 80 BC, with seats for 20,000 spectators, or enough to hold the entire population of

Musicians play horns and a water organ *(far left)* as several pairs of combatants trade blows, supervised by men in striped tunics. Some fighters went bareheaded, while others wore helmets like the one at right.

Pompeii along with visitors from nearby communities. Sometimes the violence in the arena spilled into the stands. In AD 59 fighting broke out between Pompeians and fans from Nuceria, a neighboring town. The Nucerians were badly outmatched, and many were killed. To discourage further rowdiness, the Roman Senate exiled the individuals who started the riot and closed the Pompeii Amphitheater for 10 years, a severe punishment for the town's fervent fans.

Seating at the Pompeii Amphitheater, as at other arenas, was arranged by rank: City officials and other prominent citizens occupied the lowest rows, and average citizens sat higher up. Women had to sit in the very top rows, but they could still root vociferously for their heroes, some of whom were prized as much for their good looks as for their fighting skills. "Celadus, the Thracian, makes all the girls sigh," read one tribute to a gladiator scribbled on a wall in Pompeii. On sunny days canvas awnings were pulled out over the seats, a convenience touted in advertisements for upcoming contests. One notice in Pompeii promised bouts between gladiators as well as a "wild-animal hunt," and added that "the awnings will be used."

Often the sponsors threw a banquet for the gladiators on the night before the fights, with the public looking on. Some fighters ate sparingly, hoping to remain alert and agile for the ordeal ahead; others gorged themselves, fearing perhaps that this might be their last meal. The next day, the gladiators donned purple and gold

cloaks and paraded into the amphitheater to the cheers of the spectators. Valets followed the fighters, carrying their weapons.

To help excite the crowd for the duels that followed, men sometimes staged mock fights with wooden swords. Often, however, the appetite of the spectators had already been whetted by a morning of wild-animal shows. Some of those bloody preliminaries were close contests, as when a lion was pitted against a tiger, for example, or a man wielding a lance faced a raging bull. But other such events were mere slaughters: Unarmed criminals or captives were tied to stakes and ravaged by wild beasts, or animals were destroyed by archers from a safe distance.

The demand for beasts in the arena decimated populations of wild animals in the provinces. As early as 50 BC, when Cicero was serving as governor of Cilicia in Asia Minor, he sarcastically informed a friend who wanted panthers shipped to Roman arenas that the few panthers left in his province had grown so wary of trappers that they had absconded for a neighboring land.

The merciless animal shows sometimes lacked suspense and left spectators dazed rather than thrilled. At one event Cicero attended, large numbers of elephants were slaughtered. The spectators, while duly impressed, "showed no real enjoyment," he noted. "In fact, a certain sympathy arose for the elephants, and a feeling that there was a kind of affinity between that large animal and the human race." The historian Tacitus reported a similar response to the mass execution of Christians by Nero, who tried to deflect rumors of his own involvement in the great fire that ravaged Rome in AD 64 by blaming members of that young sect. Nero made a spectacle of their deaths, dressing some of them in animal skins and exposing them to dogs, but according to Tacitus, the bloodfest aroused only pity for the victims.

A wounded man crouches on the arena floor as two others battle lions. Unlike people condemned to be ravaged by wild beasts, bestiarii were trained and armed for the task.

Men coax an elephant and a wild ox aboard a ship in this mosaic illustrating the considerable demand for animals in Roman arenas.

However they felt about wild-animal shows, many Romans relished bouts between gladiators because they involved real skill and high drama. Attendants raked the sand to remove bloodstains before each match and periodically sprayed scented water over the crowd. Many contests pitted one type of fighter against another. A Samnite, for example, equipped with a short sword and an oblong shield, might do battle with a Thracian, carrying a scimitar and a round shield. Or a *murmillo,* wearing a helmet with a prominent fish crest, dueled with sword and shield against a bareheaded retiarius, armed with a net, a trident, and a dagger.

A trumpeter signaled the start of the match, and the deadly dance that followed was accompanied by the piping of flutes, the rattle of drums, and the lugubrious tones of a water organ. Each time a gladiator fell, the trumpet sounded anew and the crowd roared. To ensure that the men put up a good fight, an instructor stood by yelling "Strike!" and "Slay!" and brandishing a whip or a hot iron to enforce his commands. Although the fighting was furious, it was not always fatal. Some matches ended in a draw, and a faltering fighter was often given a chance to appeal for mercy by casting aside his weapons and raising his left hand in supplication. His fate rested in the hands of the presiding host—usually the emperor himself at the Colosseum. But even the emperor was expected to defer to the opinion of the crowd, who put their thumbs up or down to signal their verdict.

Spectators often spared combatants who fought bravely but condemned those who ran from their opponents or groveled for mercy. "We hate those weak and suppliant gladiators," wrote Cicero, "who, hands outstretched, beseech us to let them live." If the verdict was death, the winner performed the execution promptly, and the body was removed by attendants through a gate for the dead. Then the emperor rewarded the victor—often in the form of silver dishes brimming with gold pieces. As with the charioteers, part if not all of the winnings went to the gladiator's owner.

An inscription in Pompeii recorded the results

POET IN SEARCH OF PATRONS

Unlike the Greeks, the Romans did not regularly include contests in poetry among their games. Roman poets inspired by the divine muses *(below)* had to seek worldly success in other ways, often vying for the support of patrons. The emperor Augustus and his wealthy confidant Maecenas patronized some brilliant writers, including the epic poet Virgil, a farmer's son who extolled the glory of Rome and its rulers. But talent was not always rewarded in high places. The gifted poet Ovid ran afoul of Augustus on moral grounds and was banished. And the sharp satirist Juvenal, who was born during Nero's reign, resented the patronage system and lambasted the leaders of society for their decadence and depravity.

VIRGIL

Virgil swore he had begun the writing of his masterwork, the *Aeneid,* in a fit of insanity. By 19 BC he had labored on his poem exalting the origins and destiny of the Romans for 11 years. A meticulous writer, he felt it needed more work. But while traveling in Greece, he fell mortally ill, and reportedly ordered his epic to be destroyed. But Augustus, having heard part of the poem, denied his final wish—thus saving one of the treasures of Western literature.

> *and Romulus, rejoicing*
> *In the brown wolf-skin of his*
> *foster-mother,*
> *Takes up the tribe, and builds the*
> *martial walls*
> *And calls the people, after himself,*
> *the Romans.*
> *To these I set no bounds in space*
> *or time;*
> *They shall rule forever.—Aeneid*

OVID

At age 19 the aristocratic Ovid defied his father's wishes, abandoning politics to devote himself to poetry. Fashionable Romans embraced him and quoted his erotic verses on city walls. But Ovid was not just a love poet—his greatest work, the *Metamorphoses,* dealt with mythological themes. Still, Augustus exiled the poet in AD 8. Ovid died in a dreary Black Sea outpost nine years later, still longing for home.

> *Tacticians recommend the night attack,*
> *use of the spearhead,*
> *catching the foe asleep.*
> *These tactics wiped out Rhesus*
> *and his Thracians,*
> *capturing the famous horses.*
> *Lovers use them too—to exploit*
> *a sleeping husband,*
> *thrusting hard while the enemy snores,*
> *eluding guards and night patrols,*
> *moving under cover.—Amores*

JUVENAL

Unlike Virgil and Ovid, Juvenal, reportedly the son of a wealthy freedman, did not enjoy renown in his lifetime. And the satires he composed left posterity with a vivid impression of a man at odds with his times. In them Juvenal accused the Roman people of hypocrisy, extortion, sexual excess, greed, and cruelty—not to mention a shameless fascination with the heroes of the stage, circus, and arena. In the corrupt society bitterly portrayed by Juvenal, aristocratic women run off with gladiators, rulers admit actors and their cronies to high office, and the public cares only for games and giveaways.

> *The people that once bestowed commands, consulships, legions, and all else, now concerns itself no more, and longs eagerly for just two things—bread and circuses!—Satire X*

of one day at the arena: In nine matches involving 18 gladiators, three losers died in defeat; the other six escaped with their lives. Fans were naturally reluctant to condemn one of their favorites simply because he had a bad outing now and then. Severus, for example, won 13 matches before losing to a gladiator named Albanus. Evidently, the spectators felt he had earned a reprieve, and he justified their faith in him by resuming his winning ways.

Most gladiators were forced into the arena, having been raised as slaves, captured in battle, or condemned as criminals. Occasionally, impoverished freedmen signed on as gladiators for a fixed term. A few women fought as well, but largely as novelties. Slaves were freed from the obligation to continue fighting by earning the coveted *rudis*, a wooden sword granted to gifted gladiators at the whim of the emperor or presiding official. But the lure of the arena was strong for successful gladiators, and some who were free to leave stayed on.

Despite the lowly origins of most gladiators, some men of high rank envied their feats and freely entered the arena themselves. One of Nero's predecessors, Caligula, enjoyed trading blows with professional gladiators in practice sessions, although the fighters themselves must have dreaded the bouts. It was said that during one such match, Caligula's sparring partner, armed with only a wooden sword, fell down on purpose so that the emperor could claim a win, whereupon Caligula drew a dagger and stabbed him to death.

Caligula's fondness for fighting was tame compared to that of Commodus, who reigned toward the end of the second century AD. Some found it hard to believe that he was the natural son of Marcus Aurelius, a philosophical ruler who disliked blood sports. By one account, Commodus was conceived after his mother, Faustina, fell violently in love with a gladiator she glimpsed from a distance. The worried Marcus Aurelius reportedly consulted soothsayers, who told him that "this gladiator should be killed and that Faustina should bathe in his blood and afterward lie with her husband. When this advice had been followed, the empress' passion was in fact spent, but she brought into the world Commodus, who was more of a gladiator than a prince."

Many Roman theaters had spectacular stage scenery, as shown by a wall painting of a backdrop *(above)* and a model of Rome's Marcellus Theater *(right)*, whose ornate, multistoried set had three entrances for actors. The central doorway was for characters that were emerging from the palace, while those on either side were for characters arriving from the country or town.

Whatever the origins of Commodus's enthusiasm for fighting, it grew into a mania. Before he was assassinated at the age of 31 in AD 192, the emperor reportedly dueled against more than a thousand opponents and won every time, for no one dared to defeat him. He never seriously harmed his opponents in public competition. But in private bouts at his home, according to one of his contemporaries, the senator and historian Dio Cassius, Commodus killed or maimed more than a few of his foes, slicing off "the noses of some, the ears of others, and sundry features of still others."

The emperor also liked to participate in the slaughter of wild animals, downing as many as 100 bears at a time from the safety of a platform. He modeled himself after Hercules, the slayer of beasts, and like his hero, sported a lion skin and a club. Senators were summoned to watch him perform in the arena and had to hail him in unison. "Thou art lord and thou art first!" they proclaimed on cue. "Of all men most fortunate! Victor thou art!" At times they found it hard to keep a straight face. Once, when Commodus severed the head of an ostrich and raised it triumphantly, Dio Cassius and other onlookers picked bitter laurel leaves from their garlands and chewed them furiously to keep from erupting in laughter—an outburst that could have been fatal.

The antics of deluded rulers were not the only theatrical performances in town. Romans had a gift for satire and mimicry and expressed that talent in stage shows that were farcical, frenetic, and hugely popular. Rome also nurtured some serious playwrights, but they had difficulty competing for public attention

even in the simpler days of the Republic, when the taste for lavish spectacles was not yet fully developed.

Terence, a writer of the second century BC who composed artful comedies in elegant verse inspired by Greek drama, did his best to keep his audience from being distracted by less sophisticated forms of entertainment. For the third production of his play *The Mother-in-Law,* he wrote a wry prologue in which the producer walked on stage to introduce the drama and urged spectators not to flee the theater for simpler treats. At the first production of the play, the producer complained, crowds had gathered nearby to watch boxers compete and a tightrope walker perform, and the resulting commotion forced the actors off the stage before the play was finished. At the second performance, he added, the audience heard that some gladiators were about to perform elsewhere and flew off in a rush to see blood spilled. The producer begged the audience to hear the actors out this time: "Don't allow, by your neglect, music and drama to fade away, appreciated by only a few."

Despite such urgings, classical drama lost out in the competition for spectators. In imperial times, plays of literary sophistication like the tragedies written by Nero's tutor Seneca were usually recited before private gatherings of wealthy and well-educated Romans. Most peo-

Two actors in goatskin loincloths rehearse with others for a satyr play *(left).* A tradition that originated in Greece, satirical drama remained popular in Rome, where actors often adhered to the classical custom of wearing masks, as portrayed on the statue at right.

ple favored shows of greater visual appeal. Many of the productions had no dialogue at all, relying instead for dramatic effect on the gestures of the actors. Nearly as popular as such pantomimes were the mime plays, whose success often had as much to do with the ingenious scenic effects as with the clever lines the actors spoke. Some of these productions dealt with mythological themes and others addressed the misadventures of stock characters—lovesick youths, knavish slaves, boastful soldiers, miserly old men, and shrewish wives.

More days were devoted to such shows during games than to chariot races or gladiatorial bouts. According to the Roman historian Livy, the first theatrical performances in the capital were staged in 364 BC in an attempt to please the gods and bring an end to a plague. In later times Romans continued to honor the gods theatrically by parading an eagle representing Jupiter or a dove representing Venus from the temple to the theater. As at the circuses and amphitheaters, spectators arrived early for the performances and stayed late, since one show might follow another throughout the day.

To accommodate the eager multitudes, Romans built large theaters. Some early structures, constructed wholly or partly of wood, held as many as 20,000 spectators. Pompey's Theater, a durable structure of stone dedicated in 55 BC, had at least 10,000 seats. Given the scale of these buildings, it was no wonder that Nero tried to strengthen his voice for the stage. The permanent stone theaters were semicircular in shape, with a covered stage. Dignitaries sat up front, and common people farther back, but the seating rules were sometimes defied. In 41 BC a group of soldiers threatened the future emperor Augustus after he ordered one of their comrades arrested for daring to sit near the front.

Theatergoers were entranced by wondrous backdrops and special effects—ghosts emerging from trapdoors and gods supported by artfully disguised cranes soaring across the heavens. But not all the thrills were make-believe. Perhaps to compete with chariot races or wild-animal shows, those who sponsored the performances sometimes transformed theaters into circuses. In one production, extras rode horses across the stage to dramatize the sacking of a city. In another, 600 mules stole the show. Some sponsors went further and imitated the bloodshed in the arena by arranging for criminals or captives to be sacrificed on stage. At the end of one show, a victim portraying Hercules was burned to death. In another grisly climax that may have been either accidental or planned, a man playing the part of Icarus, the mythical figure who flew too close to the sun on wings of wax, plunged to his death, splattering blood on Nero as he watched.

In the theater as in the arena, spectators were free with their opinions, sometimes waving their handkerchiefs or the flaps of their togas to express approval. They could be just as effusive with their criticism, however, occasionally booing players off the stage with yells of "Bring on the bears!" Sponsors tried to stifle such outbursts by paying people to lead applause at their plays, no matter how dismal the performance. Such rhythmic clapping could be quite appealing—more so, perhaps, than the show itself.

For all the tricks and stunts, success in the theater still rested on the ability of the performers to stir the emotions of their audience. Even the wordless art of pantomime required great eloquence on the actor's part. In some shows, a single *pantomimus* (one who imitates everything), supported by a chorus and musicians, played the parts of all the characters. "Their hands demand and promise," wrote the Roman orator Quintilian of the great pantomime artists, "they summon and dismiss. . . . To suggest illness, they imitate the doctor feeling the patient's pulse; to indicate music they spread their fingers in the fashion of a lyre."

Pantomime shows were essentially dances. Apuleius, a writer of the second century AD, described one such exotic performance in his fictional work, *The Golden Ass*. The drama represented the judgment of Paris, who had to choose among three goddesses—Juno, Minerva, and Venus—and award the golden apple to the most beautiful. Venus appeared before Paris naked, Apuleius wrote, except for a silk scarf that "covered,

Wearing a leering mask much like the one above, an actor playing a slave *(far right)* helps a drunken youth find his way home from a rollicking party while a flute player serenades them. Across the stage, danger lurks in the form of the young man's irate father, staff in hand. The characters' masks identified them as stock comic types.

or rather shaded, her quite remarkable hips and which an inquisitive wind mischievously either blew aside or sometimes pressed clingingly against her." Two groups of women representing the Graces and the Seasons joined her on the stage, scattering flowers and dancing around her to the sweet tunes of flutes. Venus then moved forward, swaying gently and "answering the tender sound of the flutes with her delicate movements." Thoroughly entranced, Paris granted her the prize.

Although female roles were traditionally played by men wearing wigs and makeup or masks, there were more than a few women on stage by imperial times. They might

Performers frolic in this Roman mosaic. Music and dance were especially important for pantomime artists, who expressed themselves with movements rather than words.

be touted for their talent and beauty, but they were still considered disreputable—as were their male counterparts. Most actors were either freedmen or slaves. Some won freedom and fame through their talents, but those who rose too high might come crashing back to earth like the fabled Icarus. The celebrated actor Mnester, for example, was executed along with Messalina, the third wife of Claudius, after the emperor learned that Mnester had served as an accomplice to Messalina in her affair with another man. Another vaunted actor named Paris was stalked and killed in the street by Domitian after that emperor found that his wife was in love with the performer.

Women who took to acting and were derided as prostitutes were simply following in the footsteps of their notorious brethren.

At least one well-to-do woman named Ummidia Quadratilla was so enamored of the theater that she purchased a troupe of performers and hired them out to festival organizers. Other wealthy Romans enjoyed popular drama as much as she did, but it was unusual for an aristocratic woman to involve herself in the business. Quadratilla was a widow, however, and she needed something to help fill her idle hours, which were largely devoted to the playing of draughts, an early form of checkers.

Her theatrical career was described by Pliny the Younger in a letter written after her death at the age of 78. Pliny considered her involvement with the troupe "an indulgence unsuitable for a lady of her high position." But he gave her credit for not exposing her grandson, a handsome and morally upright young man called Quadratus, who grew up in her home, to the actors. "Quadratus never watched performances either in the theater or at home, nor did she insist on it," Pliny wrote. Whenever Quadratilla hosted her players, he added, she sent her grandson out of the room to study.

Only once, shortly before his grandmother's death, did Quadratus see a performance of her troupe. Pliny attended the show with him. "People who were nothing to Quadratilla were running to the theater to pay their respects to her," he wrote, "though 'respect' is hardly the word to use for their fawning attentions—jumping up and clapping to show their admiration, and then copying every gesture of their mistress with snatches of song." Pliny, a noted public figure, could scarcely imagine what it meant

Two clay figurines—one holding a dagger, the other clutching a money bag—represent the farcical characters of the humorous and antic mime plays.

to Quadratilla to receive such recognition, even from lowly actors and their fans. He seemed pleased that she bequeathed the bulk of her estate to her grandson and left her theatrical retainers "only a tiny bequest as a gratuity for their hired applause."

The disapproval that Pliny expressed for Quadratilla's venture was nothing compared to the contempt aristocratic Romans felt for Nero when he took to the stage. Perhaps Nero's compulsive showmanship was an attempt to overcome the insecurity he felt as a young man, thrust into power at the age of 16 and manipulated by his elders, in particular his scheming mother, Agrippina, and his exacting tutor Seneca. By garnering prize after prize for his performances, Nero tried to show that he could stand on his own and command esteem. Yet the victories rang hollow, and no amount of contrived applause slaked his hunger for approval.

Surprisingly for a ruler who was virtually assured of winning any competition he entered, Nero suffered from stage fright and dreaded criticism. "Before every performance he would address the judges with the utmost deference: saying that he had done what he could, and that the issue was now in Fortune's hands," Suetonius related. Some of the judges urged him not to worry, but others were too embarrassed to speak, and he mistook their silence for "alienation and disfavor." Once, while acting in a competition, he dropped his scepter and almost gave up, fearing disqualification. But the accompanist who was playing the flute as he performed reassured him by claiming that the "slip had passed unnoticed, because the audience were listening with such rapt attention." So tender was Nero's self-esteem that no one could leave the theater while he was performing, however great the emergency. Pregnant women reportedly remained in their seats after the onset of labor and gave birth there; men nearly bored to death feigned the real thing and were carried out for burial.

It was largely the upper classes who suffered such travails and worse under Nero. He remained popular with the lower classes and may have felt for a while that the hostile aristocrats were no threat. After all, members of the senatorial order wielded far less power in Rome than they once had. But they remained a force to be reckoned with, particularly in their capacity as provincial governors and commanders. In time Nero became the target of conspiracies involving Romans of high rank. In AD 66, after the discovery of one such plot, he had three commanders of senatorial rank killed. Two years later, Nero's fate was sealed when provincial leaders took arms against him, first in Gaul and later in Spain and Africa.

Ultimately, Suetonius reported, the prefect of Nero's guard deserted him, and he lost hope. A Roman in his position was expected to die by his own hand, but Nero found it hard to follow the script. In desperation he called for a gladiator named Spiculus to come and put an end to him, but neither Spiculus nor anyone else wanted to play the part of executioner. After taking refuge in the home of his freedman, Phaon, Nero learned to his horror that the Senate had declared him a public enemy, fit to be punished in "ancient style," which meant being stripped naked and flogged to death with rods. "How ugly and vulgar my life has become!" Nero lamented. Finally, with the help of his secretary, he managed to stab himself fatally in the throat.

Shortly before his death, Nero tearfully expressed regret that his enemies, in driving him to suicide, were depriving society of "so great an artist!" He believed that the Roman theater would never see his like again, and in a sense he was right. But the games went on without him, and Rome remained great on the world stage in a way that transcended the feats or follies of any single performer.

A seated statue of Sabina, wife of the emperor Hadrian, seems to gaze out over the ruin of a still impressive Roman theater in North Africa—an enduring legacy of a culture that dominated the vast arena of the Mediterranean world for centuries.

GLOSSARY

Advocate: a skilled speaker, trained in the law, who presented the case of a party at a Roman trial.

Aediles: four annually elected officials with responsibility during the republic for Rome's public games and buildings, streets, markets, and the grain supply. By the early empire the management of the games and grain supply had been transferred to other officials. Other Roman towns also had aediles. The name comes from *aedes*, meaning temple structure.

Amphitheater: an oval building designed for the staging of gladiatorial and animal spectacles.

Apollo: a Greek deity also worshiped by Romans as the god of healing, hunting, prophecy, and poetry. Augustus considered Apollo his patron and promoted his worship.

Aqueduct: a man-made conduit for supplying water, usually constructed of stone with a cement lining and running at or below ground level or over bridges. The water was fed to fountains, bathhouses, private homes, mills, and irrigation systems.

Arena: from *harena*, meaning sand; the open, sanded area in an amphitheater or circus, where combats, shows, and races took place.

Augurs: the official diviners of Rome, organized in their own priestly college to which they were elected for life. The augurs interpreted signs from the gods to determine if an upcoming event, such as a military campaign, would meet with divine approval, and they also announced unsolicited portents of doom.

Auxiliaries: troops recruited from Rome's allies and client states. Rome increasingly relied on auxiliaries to supply its cavalry; auxiliaries also played important roles as light infantry and specialist troops.

Century: the smallest unit of the Roman army, with a nominal strength of 100 men, though the actual number varied; commanded by a centurion.

Ceres: a Roman earth goddess associated with grain and identified with the Greek goddess Demeter; patroness of farmers.

Circus: a building designed mainly for chariot racing.

Cithara: an elaborate type of lyre.

City prefect: as instituted by Augustus, the official responsible for maintaining order in Rome. The city prefect commanded the city police force and presided over his own court of law. The position was reserved for men of senatorial status.

Client: a man who entered into a dependent relationship with a patron, offering him political support and attending on him at home and in public, in return for protection and such benefits as food or money.

Cloaca: a drain or sewer.

Collegium: an association, club, or guild. Rome's major priesthoods were organized into collegia, as were many trades. Burial, sports, and veterans' associations could also be found throughout the Roman world.

Colonnaded: architectural term for a continuous row of columns.

Consul: the top military and civil official of the republic. Two consuls were elected to serve simultaneously for a one-year period. Though still prestigious, the consulship offered little real power in the imperial age. The term of office was shortened, and emperors held the consulship themselves or filled it with their friends and relatives.

Denarius: the standard silver coin of Rome from the middle republic until the later imperial period, by which time its silver content had drastically declined.

Dictator: during the republic, an official appointed to exercise supreme authority during a crisis, for a period of up to six months. By the first century BC, Roman politicians were using the position to control the government.

Dionysus: Greek god of wine, theater, and fertility, whose Roman counterpart was Bacchus. Though regarded as the bringer of joy, Dionysus also had a dark side associated with death, madness, and violence. He was sometimes represented by a mask on a column, or was depicted as a young man bearing a drinking cup and a grapevine.

Duumviri municipales: the two highest-ranking officials in colonies and municipal governments under Roman rule, responsible for overseeing the local councils. They typically served for one year.

Equestrian order: the order of business-oriented Roman landowners ranking below the senatorial order; its members engaged in finance, trade, agriculture, public contracting, and tax collection but generally did not directly involve themselves in politics. Under the empire, equestrians served as military officers and bureaucrats. The name comes from *equites*, which originally referred to members of the cavalry, in turn derived from *equus*, meaning horse.

Etruscans: the inhabitants of ancient Etruria, an area in north central Italy organized into a loose confederation of 12 city-states that dominated much of Italy culturally and militarily before the rise of Rome.

Forum: a large, open area, typically rectangular in shape and surrounded by public buildings, which served as the political, social, and commercial center of a Roman town. Large cities, such as Rome, often had more than one forum.

Freedman/freedwoman: a slave who had been freed by his or her master. Roman law provided for most to become citizens. Although not eligible for major political offices, freedmen figured prominently in the imperial bureaucracy in the first century AD.

Garum: a strong fish sauce made by fermenting intestines and other fish parts for several months. Mackerel was popular; other types of fish used included anchovies, sprats, and tuna.

Graces: minor female deities personifying charm, grace, and beauty, usually three in number when depicted in classical art and literature.

Ides: the 15th day of a month with 31 days, or the 13th day in other months.

Imperator: "emperor"; during the republic, a victorious general was hailed "imperator" by his troops and subsequently used the title with his name until his triumphal procession in Rome. Augustus received the title from the Senate in 29 BC and made it a permanent part of his name. The title came to signify the supreme ruler.

Insula: "island"; a multistory tenement, typically with shops and workrooms on the ground floor and apartments on the upper floors, all built around a central courtyard. The term is also sometimes applied to a block of such buildings. The insula was the most common form of housing in Rome during the imperial age.

Isis: a deity of Egyptian origin whose symbol was the cow. By Roman times Isis was regarded as a goddess of fertility, maternity, and marriage. Her cult reached Rome during the late republic and soon spread throughout the empire.

Juno: Jupiter's wife and one of Rome's major civic deities, identified with the Greek goddess Hera and associated with marriage, fertility, and childbirth.

Jupiter: supreme deity of the Roman pantheon and protector of Rome, symbolized by a scepter; his Greek counterpart was Zeus.

Legion: the largest unit in the Roman army; the number and size of legions varied over time.

Legionary legate: under the empire, the commanding officer of an individual legion in the provinces; the legate was from the senatorial class.

Ludi: "games"; the term for chariot races and theatrical, gladiatorial, and animal shows and contests held in Rome in connection with religious festivals.

Lyre: a musical instrument with vertical strings that were plucked with the fingers or struck with a plectrum, an implement made of bone, wood, or horn.

Macedonia: homeland of Alexander the Great, from which he conquered an empire extending from Asia Minor and Egypt to India. One of Alexander's generals, Ptolemy, established Egypt's Macedonian royal house in the late fourth century BC. Macedonia itself became a Roman province in the mid-second century BC.

Mars: the god of war, identified with the Greek god Ares. He was regarded as the son of Juno and was second only to Jupiter in importance.

Mime: a popular theatrical form typically featuring farcical plots, stock characters, and bawdy dialogue and action. Both men and women performed as mimes.

Minerva: goddess of crafts and trade guilds, identified with the Greek goddess Athena. She was also regarded as a goddess of wisdom and war.

Munera: a general term for duties or obligations of a personal or public nature, applied specifically to early gladiatorial contests staged to honor the dead.

Nobles: from *nobiles*, meaning well known; members of families with ancestors who had held high office in Rome, in particular the consulship.

Novus homo: literally, "new man." The label was applied during the late republic to the first man of a family to serve in the Senate, and in particular to those few men, such as Cicero, who attained the consulship despite their nonsenatorial family origins.

Optimates: the "best" men: the traditionalist faction in the Senate during the late republic; notable optimates included Cicero and Cato the Younger.

Pantomime: a popular dramatic form in which a dancer interpreted a story through gesture and movement alone, with backing from a chorus and orchestra. Most performers wore masks.

Papyrus: a tall marsh plant, and the paperlike sheets made from it. Papyrus was manufactured and sold in rolls. Originating in Egypt, papyrus became the most widespread writing material in the Roman world.

Pater Patriae: an honorific title meaning father of the country, granted by the Senate beginning in the first century BC. Augustus had the title bestowed on him in 2 BC; most subsequent emperors also received it.

Patricians: an elite collection of landed families that controlled politics, the state religion, and the courts in the early republic. Although the patricians were forced to share power with the plebeians, they remained the dominant political class until the end of the republic.

Patron: a man of influence who undertakes to provide legal and financial aid to his clients (comprising both his former slaves and freeborn men of lesser means who have attached themselves to him) in return for their political support and regular attendance on him in public and private.

Pietas: the dutiful respect Romans were expected to accord to their gods, parents, commanders, and rulers.

Plebeians: term for Roman citizens who did not belong to the exclusive patrician class.

Populares: the "supporters of the people"; the faction in the Senate that sought reform by appealing to popular opinion; opponents of the optimates.

Portico: an open or partially closed porch or walk with a roof supported by columns.

Praetorian Guard: the emperor's bodyguard, established by Augustus in 27 BC. The elite Rome-based force played a central role in the politics of the empire, making and unmaking many of Rome's imperial rulers.

Praetorian prefect: title of the commander of the Praetorian Guard. Over time the prefects took on major political, judicial, and administrative responsibilities in addition to their military duties, becoming second only to the emperor in importance.

Princeps: "first citizen"; an unofficial title chosen by Augustus and assumed by his successors at their accession.

Province: a geographically defined area outside Italy administered by a governor from Rome. During the empire some provinces were administered by the Senate while others were under the emperor's control.

Punic: Carthaginian; from the Latin word for the Phoenicians, who founded Carthage.

Rostra: the speaker's platform in the Forum, which took its name from the prows (rostra) of enemy ships with which it was decorated.

Samnites: a warlike people inhabiting south central Italy who contested Roman supremacy for much of the republican period. The name Samnite was also applied to a type of gladiator who wore a visored helmet and carried a sword and shield.

Sarcophagus: from the Greek, meaning flesh eater; a coffin, usually made of stone, for burial of the dead. Burial replaced cremation as the prevailing method of disposing of the dead in Rome during the second and third centuries AD.

Senate: effectively, the governing body of Rome during the republic, composed of ex-officials from patrician and, later, wealthy plebeian, families, who served for life. Though its formal role was consultative, the Senate exercised great power over Rome's officials and assemblies. During the imperial age the Senate's power was considerably diminished and membership was extended to the provincial elite.

Sestertius: a widely circulated coin worth one quarter of a denarius. Production of sesterces ceased in the third century AD.

Strigil: a curved implement of bronze, iron, or bone used after bathing to scrape sweat, oil, and dead skin from the body.

Stoics: adherents of a Greek school of philosophy founded in Athens around 300 BC. Stoic doctrine emphasized detachment from the outer world, in accordance with the belief that a divine providence determined all of existence.

Stylus: a writing tool made of bone, bronze, or iron, with a pointed end for incising letters on wax tablets and a flattened end for rubbing the wax smooth.

Taberna: a shop or office, typically one room with a wide door opening onto a street or courtyard. The display space and work area was up front; the back of the room or a mezzanine floor was used for storage and living quarters.

Toga: the standard outer garment of Roman citizens, semicircular in shape and made of wool. Togas were generally five to six yards long and three to four yards wide and were worn draped around the body and over the shoulder without fasteners.

Tribunes of the people: annually elected officers of the plebeians who protected their rights, lives, and property. The tribunes gained veto power over laws, elections, and officials' acts and were immune from prosecution. Rome's emperors assumed the tribunes' powers or delegated them to their preferred heirs.

Triumph: the celebratory procession awarded to a victorious Roman general. Traditionally, the purple-garbed general rode in an ornate four-horse chariot through Rome to the Temple of Jupiter, with soldiers, officials, notable captives, spoils, and sacrificial animals in his train.

Triumvirate: a governing body of three men. During the republic three-men boards were used for such functions as founding colonies and supervising the minting of coins. The most famous triumvirates were the First Triumvirate of Caesar, Pompey, and Crassus, and the Second Triumvirate of Octavian, Antony, and Lepidus.

Vandals: a warlike Germanic people who migrated from the Baltic to modern Hungary by the middle of the second century AD; in the early fifth century they overran Gaul and Spain and sacked Rome, ultimately settling and founding their own kingdom in North Africa. The Byzantine Empire conquered the Vandals in the early sixth century AD.

Venationes: "hunts"; name applied to the display and slaughter of animals, one of the most popular Roman spectacles. The animals were hunted by other animals or by human fighters, or were set loose upon criminals or captives.

Venus: goddess of love in the Roman pantheon, affiliated with the Greek goddess Aphrodite.

Via: a broad thoroughfare; roads bearing this designation typically connected Rome to other towns.

Villa: originally, the term for a farmstead associated with an estate, comprising both farm buildings and quarters for the visiting landowner; by the second century BC the term was also applied to the countryseats of wealthy Romans.

Visigoths: the West Goths; a Germanic people who settled in Dacia, north of the Danube, by the early fourth century AD. Under pressure from the Huns, the Visigoths slashed through Greece and Italy, sacking Rome itself in 410 AD.

ACKNOWLEDGMENTS

The editors wish to thank the following individuals and institutions for their valuable assistance in the preparation of this volume:

Maria Rosaria Borriello, Museo Archeologico Nazionale, Naples, Italy; Jacklyn Burns, The J. Paul Getty Museum, Malibu, California; Dr. Caroline Dexter, George Washington University, Washington, D.C.; Hugh Elton, Trinity College, Hartford, Conn.; Pedar Foss, University of Cincinnati, Cincinnati, Ohio; Gerda Green-Marquardt, Römisch-Germanisches Museum, Köln, Germany; Heidrun Klein, Bildarchiv Preussischer Kulturbesitz, Berlin, Germany; Marie Montembault, Département des Antiquités Grecques et Romaines, Musée du Louvre, Paris, France; Tamara Palombi, Associazione Nazionale Cooperativi di Consumatori, Rome, Italy; Thomas Zühmer, Rheinisches Landesmuseum, Trier, Germany.

PICTURE CREDITS

The sources for the illustrations that appear in this volume are listed below. Credits from left to right are separated by semicolons; from top to bottom they are separated by dashes.

Cover: Photo RMN-R.G. Ojeda/Louvre, Paris.

1-5: Alfredo & Pio Foglia, Naples/Museo Archeologico Nazionale, Naples. **6-7:** Fabio Muzzi, Ghezzano (PI). **8-11:** Background by John Drummond, Time-Life Books. **12, 13:** Maps by John Drummond, Time-Life Books. **14, 15:** Eberhard Thiem, Lotos Film, Kaufbeuren. **16, 17:** Trustees of the British Museum, London; Scala, Florence; Scala, Florence/Musei Vaticani, Rome. **18:** Lauros-Giraudon, Paris. **19:** Alfredo & Pio Foglia, Naples. **20:** Scala, Florence/Museo Archeologico Nazionale, Naples. **21:** Araldo De Luca, Rome. **22:** Alfredo & Pio Foglia, Naples. **23:** Trustees of the British Museum, London—Araldo De Luca, Rome; Alfredo & Pio Foglia, Naples (2). **24:** Giraudon, Paris; Gianni Dagli Orti, Paris—Trustees of the British Museum, London. **25:** Michael Holford, Loughton, Essex—Alfredo & Pio Foglia, Naples. **26:** Michael Holford, Loughton, Essex. **27:** Trustees of the British Museum, London. **29:** Giovanni Lattanzi, Giulianova (TE); Araldo De Luca, Rome. **30:** Eberhard Thiem, Lotos Film, Kaufbeuren; Nimatallah/Artephot, Paris. **32:** Alfredo & Pio Foglia, Naples. **33:** Roger-Viollet, Paris/Museo della Civiltà Romana, Rome. **35:** Eberhard Thiem, Lotos Film, Kaufbeuren; Trustees of the British Museum, London (2). **36:** Bildarchiv Preussischer Kulturbesitz, Berlin, courtesy of Museo Prenestino, Palestrina/photo by Alfredo Dagli Orti. **37:** ALEA/Robert Steven Bianchi. **39:** Araldo De Luca, Rome—Roger-Viollet, Paris/Museo delle Terme, Rome. **40:** Scala, Florence/Museo Archeologico Nazionale, Naples. **41:** Scala, Florence/Museo Archeologico Nazionale, Naples; Lauros-Giraudon, Paris/Louvre, Paris. **42:** Scala, Florence/Musei Vaticani, Rome—Archiv für Kunst und Geschichte, Berlin, photo Erich Lessing/Museo Archeologico Nazionale, Naples. **43:** Alfredo & Pio Foglia/Museo Archeologico Nazionale, Naples. **44:** Alfredo & Pio Foglia, Naples—RMN/Louvre, Paris. **46:** Gianni Dagli Orti, Paris/Museo Capitolino, Rome. **47:** Staatliche Sammlung Ägyptischer Kunst, Munich. **48, 49:** Alfredo & Pio Foglia, Naples. **50:** Alfredo & Pio Foglia, Naples. **51:** The Metropolitan Museum of Art, Rogers Fund, 1903 (03.14.13), photograph by Schecter Lee. **52:** The Metropolitan Museum of Art, Rogers Fund, 1903 (03.14.13). **53:** Scala/Art Resource, New York; Alfredo & Pio Foglia, Naples—Mimmo Jodice, Naples. **54:** Michael Holford, Loughton, Essex. **55:** Alinari-Giraudon/Museo Archeologico Nazionale, Naples—Alfredo & Pio Foglia, Naples. **56:** Alfredo & Pio Foglia/Museo Archeologico Nazionale, Naples; Scala/Art Resource, New York. **57:** The J. Paul Getty Museum, Malibu, California, photograh by Charles Passela, Main Peristyle Garden, number 2015. **58:** Photo RMN, Paris. **60:** Nimatallah/Artephot, Paris/Museo Archeologico Nazionale, Naples. **62, 63:** The J. Paul Getty Museum, Malibu, California, No. 79.AG.112, unknown artist, *Fresco with Preparation of a Meal*, third quarter of first century AD, Fresco, H: 68.5cm; W: 122cm. **65:** Araldo De Luca, Rome; Scala, Florence/Musei Vaticani, Rome. **66, 67:** Background Michael Holford, Loughton, Essex. **66:** Scala, Florence. **67:** Alfredo & Pio Foglia, Naples; Michael Holford, Loughton, Essex—Alfredo & Pio Foglia, Naples—Trustees of the British Museum, London (4). **68:** Rheinisches Landesmuseum, Trier, photo by Thomas Zühmer. **69:** Mimmo Jodice, Naples. **70:** Michael Holford, Loughton, Essex—C.M. Dixon, Canterbury, Kent. **71:** Copyright Andromeda Oxford Limited, Abingdon, Oxfordshire. **72:** Bildarchiv Preussischer Kulturbesitz, Berlin/Museo Archeologico, Venice/photo by Alfredo Dagli Orti, 1993. **73:** Trustees of the British Museum, London. **74:** Gianni Dagli Orti, Paris/Louvre, Paris. **75:** Photo Hubert Josse, Paris. **76, 77:** Trustees of the British Museum, London, except relief, Stephen Natanson/Musei Vaticani, Rome. **78, 79:** Scala, Florence (women)—Gianni Dagli Orti, Paris/Musée d'Archéologie, Timgad, Algeria; Gemeinnützige Stiftung Leonard von Matt; Gianni Dagli Orti, Paris/Museo della Civiltà Romana, Rome. **80, 81:** Trustees of the British Museum, London; Ancient Art and Architecture Collection, Pinner, Middlesex; Alfredo & Pio Foglia, Naples. **82:** Araldo De Luca, Rome. **83:** Araldo De Luca, Rome; A. Dagli Orti/I.G.D.A., Milan/Museo della Civiltà Romana, Rome. **84:** Mimmo Jodice, Naples. **85:** Nimatallah/Artephot, Paris/Museo Archeologico Nazionale, Naples—Michael Freeman/Guildhall Museum, London. **86:** © Erich Lessing, Culture and Fine Arts Archive, Vienna. **87:** Scala, Florence/Museo Archeologico Nazionale, Naples. **89:** Claus Hansmann, Munich/courtesy Prähistorische Staatssammlung, Munich; Scala, Florence/Museo Nazionale, Ravenna. **90:** Alfredo & Pio Foglia, Naples—Michael Holford, Loughton, Essex. **91:** Archiv für Kunst und Geschichte, Berlin, photo Erich Lessing/courtesy Rheinisches Landesmuseum, Trier. **92:** Gianni Dagli Orti, Paris/Museo della Civiltà Romana, Rome—Museum of London. **93:** Ralph Rainer Steffens/Bildarchiv Steffens, Mainz—Virginia Museum of Fine Arts, Richmond, Va. The Adolph D. and Wilkins C. Williams Fund. © Virginia Museum of Fine Arts, *Funerary Relief of a Potter and His Wife*, ca. AD 110, Acc. #60.2, Photo No. 38642.1-12. **94, 95:** Alinari-Giraudon/Uffizi, Florence; Scala, Florence/Museo Vaticani, Rome. **96, 97:** Archiv für Kunst und Geschichte, Berlin, photo Erich Lessing/Museo Nazionale Archeologico, Naples; Photo Bulloz, Paris; Scala, Florence/Museo Ostiense, Ostia Antica; Scala, Florence/Galleria Borghese, Rome. **98, 99:** Araldo De Luca, Rome. **100, 101:** Archiv für Kunst und Geschichte, Berlin, photo Erich Lessing/courtesy Kunsthistorisches Museum, Vienna; Alfredo & Pio Foglia, Naples. **102:** Giovanni Lattanzi, Giulianova (TE). **103:** Archiv für Kunst und Geschichte, Berlin, photo Erich Lessing/Israel Museum (IDAM), Jerusalem—Scala, Florence/Museo della Civiltà Romana, Rome. **104, 105:** Ralph Rainer Steffens/Bildarchiv Steffens, Mainz. **107-109:** C.M. Dixon, Canterbury, Kent. **110:**

RMN, Paris—Atlantide/Schapowalow, Hamburg. **111:** Trustees of the British Museum, London. **112, 113:** Laenderpress, Mainz; Römisch-Germanisches Museum, Cologne. **114, 115:** © Fred Friberg/ Robert Harding Picture Library, London; Gilles Mermet-Giraudon; C.M. Dixon, Canterbury, Kent. **116:** Archiv für Kunst und Geschichte, Berlin, photo Erich Lessing/Museo delle Terme, Rome. **117:** C.M. Dixon, Canterbury, Kent. **118:** Araldo De Luca, Rome—C.M. Dixon, Canterbury, Kent. **120, 121:** Scala/Art Resource, New York; Z. Radovan, Jerusalem. **122, 123:** Copyright the British Museum, London; Michael Freeman, London. **125:** Araldo De Luca, Rome. **126, 127:** Lauros-Giraudon/Louvre, Paris; Eberhard Thiem, Lotos Film, Kaufbeuren—Scala, Florence. **128,**

129: Scala, Florence/Antiquarium del Palatino, Rome; Alfredo & Pio Foglia/Museo Archeologico Nazionale, Naples; Scala, Florence. **130:** Eberhard Thiem, Lotos Film, Kaufbeuren. **131:** Michael Holford, Loughton, Essex; Giovanni Lattanzi, Giulianova (TE). **132, 133:** Michael Holford, Loughton, Essex. **134:** Gemeinnützige Stiftung, Leonard von Matt. **135:** Scala, Florence/Museo della Civiltà Romana, Rome. **136, 137:** Photo Hubert Josse, Paris; Araldo De Luca, Rome/Musei Capitolini, Rome. **138, 139:** Scala, Florence/ Museo delle Terme, Rome. **140, 141:** Art by John Drummond, Time-Life Books; Gianni Dagli Orti, Paris. **142, 143:** Mosaic of the Dar Buc Ammera from Zliten, second century AD, Musée des Antiquités de Tripoli, Libya (Pierre Belzeaux

from Rapho-Guillumette)—Photo Hubert Josse/ Louvre, Paris. **144, 145:** © Erich Lessing, Culture and Fine Arts Archive, Vienna; Gianni Dagli Orti, Paris/Museo delle Terme, Rome. **146, 147:** RMN/ H. Lewandowski/Louvre, Paris. **148:** Alfredo & Pio Foglia, Naples. **149:** Scala, Florence/Museo della Civiltà Romana, Rome. **150:** Alfredo & Pio Foglia, Naples. **151:** Luciano Pedicini/Museo Archeologico Nazionale, Naples. **152:** Alfredo & Pio Foglia, Naples. **153:** Nimatallah/Artephot, Paris/Museo Archeologico Nazionale, Naples. **154:** Bildarchiv Preussischer Kulturbesitz, Berlin/Museo Archeologico Nazionale, Naples/photo: Alfredo Dagli Orti. **155:** Trustees of the British Museum, London. **156:** Robert Harding Picture Library, London.

BIBLIOGRAPHY

BOOKS

Adkins, Lesley, and Roy A. Adkins:
Dictionary of Roman Religion. New York: Facts On File, 1996.
Handbook to Life in Ancient Rome. New York: Facts On File, 1994.
Ancient Portraits in the J. Paul Getty Museum (Vol. 1). Malibu, Calif.: J. Paul Getty Museum, 1987.
Andrews, Ian. *Pompeii.* Cambridge: Cambridge University Press, 1978.
Apicius. *Cookery and Dining in Imperial Rome.* Trans. by Joseph Dommers Vehling. New York: Dover, 1977.
Auguet, Roland. *Cruelty and Civilization: The Roman Games.* New York: Routledge, 1994.
Bartlett, John. *Familiar Quotations: A Collection of Passages, Phrases, and Proverbs Traced to Their Sources in Ancient and Modern Literature.* Ed. by Justin Kaplan. Boston: Little, Brown, 1992.
Bieber, Margarete. *The History of the Greek and Roman Theater.* Princeton, N.J.: Princeton University Press, 1939.
Birley, Anthony Richard:
Life in Roman Britain. New York: G. P. Putnam's Sons, 1966.
The Roman Emperor Hadrian. Haltwhistle, Northumberland, England: Barcombe, 1977.
Borriello, Maria Rosaria, et al. *Le Collezioni del Museo Nazionale di Napoli.* Rome: De Luca, 1986.
Bowman, Alan K.:
Life and Letters on the Roman Frontier. London: British Museum Press, 1994.

The Roman Writing Tablets: From Vindolanda. London: British Museum, 1983.
Bradley, Keith R.:
Discovering the Roman Family: Studies in Roman Social History. New York: Oxford University Press, 1991.
Slaves and Masters in the Roman Empire: A Study in Social Control. New York: Oxford University Press, 1987.
Breeze, David J., and Brian Dobson. *Hadrian's Wall.* London: Allen Lane, 1976.
Brewster, Ethel Hampson. *Roman Craftsmen and Tradesmen of the Early Empire.* New York: Lenox Hill, 1972 (reprint of 1917 ed.).
Brockett, Oscar G. *History of the Theatre.* Boston: Allyn and Bacon, 1991.
Bunson, Matthew. *Encyclopedia of the Roman Empire.* New York: Facts On File, 1994.
Burford, Alison. *Craftsmen in Greek and Roman Society.* New York: Cornell University Press, 1972.
Burn, Lucilla. *The British Museum Book of Greek and Roman Art.* London: British Museum Press, 1991.
Caesar, Julius. *The Conquest of Gaul (rev. ed.).* Trans. by S. A. Handford. Harmondsworth, Middlesex, England: Penguin Books, 1982.
Cameron, Alan. *Circus Factions: Blues and Greens at Rome and Byzantium.* Oxford: Clarendon Press, 1976.
Campbell, Brian. *The Roman Army, 31 BC-AD 337: A Sourcebook.* London: Routledge, 1994.
Carcopino, Jérôme. *Daily Life in Ancient Rome: The People and the City at the Height of the Empire.* Ed. by Henry T. Rowell, trans. by E. O. Lorimer. New Haven, Conn.: Yale University Press, 1962.

Cary, M., and H. H. Scullard. *A History of Rome: Down to the Reign of Constantine.* London: Macmillan Press, 1975.
Cicero, Marcus Tullius:
On Duties. Ed. by M. T. Griffin and E. M. Atkins. Cambridge: Cambridge University Press, 1991.
Selected Letters. Trans. by Shackleton Bailey. London: Penguin Books, 1986.
Clarke, John R. *The Houses of Roman Italy, 100 B.C.-A.D. 250: Ritual, Space, and Decoration.* Berkeley: University of California Press, 1991.
Clarke, M. L. *The Noblest Roman: Marcus Brutus and His Reputation.* Ithaca, N.Y.: Cornell University Press, 1981.
Connolly, Peter. *The Roman Army.* London: Macdonald, 1984.
Cordello. *Guide to the Ruins of Ostia.* Venice, Italy: Edizioni Storti, 1986.
Cornell, Tim, and John Matthews. *Atlas of the Roman World.* Oxford: Phaidon Press, 1982.
Cowell, F. R. *Life in Ancient Rome.* New York: Perigee Books, 1980.
Croft, Peter. *Roman Mythology.* London: Octopus Books, 1974.
Cunliffe, Barry:
The Roman Baths: A View over 2000 Years. Bath, England: Bath Archeological Trust, 1993.
Rome and Her Empire. London: Constable, 1994.
Dalby, Andrew, and Sally Grainger. *The Classical Cookbook.* London: British Museum Press, 1996.
Davenport, Basil, ed. *The Portable Roman Reader.* New York: Penguin Books, 1979.
Deiss, Joseph Jay:
Herculaneum: Italy's Buried Treasure. New York:

Harper & Row, 1985.

The Town of Hercules: A Buried Treasure Trove. Malibu, Calif.: J. Paul Getty Museum, 1995.

Dell'Orto, Luisa Franchi. *Roma Antica: Vita e cultura.* Florence, Italy: Scala, 1990.

Drummond, Steven K., and Lynn H. Nelson. *The Western Frontiers of Imperial Rome.* New York: M. E. Sharpe, 1994.

Duff, J. Wight:

A Literary History of Rome: From the Origins to the Close of the Golden Age. Ed. by A. M. Duff. London: Ernest Benn, 1960.

A Literary History of Rome in the Silver Age: From Tiberius to Hadrian. Ed. by A. M. Duff. London: Ernest Benn, 1964.

Dupont, Florence. *Daily Life in Ancient Rome.* Trans. by Christopher Woodall. Oxford: Blackwell, 1989.

Ellwanger, George H. *The Pleasures of the Table: An Account of Gastronomy from Ancient Days to Present Times.* Detroit: Singing Tree Press, 1969 (reprint of 1902 edition).

Etienne, Robert. *Pompeii: The Day a City Died.* London: Thames and Hudson, 1992.

Eyewitness to History. Ed. by John Carey. New York: Avon Books, 1990.

Fantham, Elaine, et al. *Women in the Classical World: Image and Text.* New York: Oxford University Press, 1994.

Freeman, Charles. *The World of the Romans.* New York: Oxford University Press, 1993.

Gardner, Jane F. *Women in Roman Law & Society.* Bloomington: Indiana University Press, 1986.

Garnsey, Peter, and Richard Saller. *The Roman Empire: Economy, Society and Culture.* Berkeley: University of California Press, 1987.

Geisinger, Marion. *Plays, Players, & Playwrights: An Illustrated History of the Theatre.* New York: Hart, 1975.

Giacosa, Ilaria Gozzini. *A Taste of Ancient Rome.* Trans. by Anna Herklotz. Chicago: University of Chicago Press, 1992.

Giannelli, Giulio, ed. *The World of Ancient Rome.* New York: Putnam, 1967.

Giardina, Andrea, ed. *The Romans.* Trans. by Lydia G. Cochrane. Chicago: University of Chicago Press, 1989.

Grant, Michael:

The Ancient Historians. New York: Charles Scribner's Sons, 1970.

Cities of Vesuvius: Pompeii and Herculaneum. New York: Penguin Books, 1978.

Cleopatra. New York: Simon and Schuster, 1972.

Gladiators. New York: Delacorte Press, 1967.

A Guide to the Ancient World: A Dictionary of Classical Place Names. New York: H. W. Wilson, 1986.

The Jews in the Roman World. New York: Charles Scribner's Sons, 1973.

The Twelve Caesars. New York: Charles Scribner's Sons, 1975.

The World of Rome. New York: Meridian, 1960.

Grant, Michael, et al. *Greece and Rome: The Birth of Western Civilization.* Ed. by Michael Grant. New York: Bonanza Books, 1986.

Grant, Michael, and Rachel Kitzinger, eds. *Civilization of the Ancient Mediterranean: Greece and Rome* (Vol. 3). New York: Charles Scribner's Sons, 1988.

Green, Peter. *Alexander to Actium: The Historical Evolution of the Hellenistic Age.* Berkeley: University of California Press, 1990.

Hadas, Moses, and the Editors of Time-Life Books. *Imperial Rome* (Great Ages of Man series). New York: Time, 1965.

Harris, H. A. *Sports in Greece and Rome.* London: Thames and Hudson, 1972.

Heinz, Werner. *Römische Thermen.* Münich: Hirmer Verlag, 1983.

Henig, Martin, ed. *A Handbook of Roman Art: A Survey of the Visual Arts of the Roman World.* Oxford: Phaidon Press, 1983.

Hibbert, Christopher. *Cities and Civilizations.* New York: Welcome Rain, 1987.

Historic World Leaders (Vol. 2). Ed. by Anne Commire. Detroit: Gale Research, 1994.

Holland, Jack, and John Monroe. *The Order of Rome.* New York: HBJ Press, 1980.

Holmes, Richard. *The World Atlas of Warfare: Military Innovations That Changed the Course of History.* New York: Viking Studio Books, 1988.

Hoobler, Dorothy, and Thomas Hoobler. *Cleopatra.* New York: Chelsea House, 1988.

Hopkins, Keith. *Conquerors and Slaves: Sociological Studies in Roman History* (Vol. 1). Cambridge, Mass.: Cambridge University Press, 1978.

Horace. *Satires, Epistles and Ars Poetica.* Trans. by H. Rushton Fairclough. London: William Heinemann, 1932.

Howatson, M. C., ed. *The Oxford Companion to Classical Literature.* Oxford: Oxford University Press, 1989.

Humphrey, John H. *Roman Circuses: Arenas for Chariot Racing.* Berkeley: University of California Press, 1986.

Huzar, Eleanor Goltz. *Mark Antony: A Biography.* Minneapolis: University of Minnesota Press, 1978.

Jackson, Donald. *The Story of Writing.* New York: Taplinger, 1981.

James, Simon. *Ancient Rome.* New York: Alfred A. Knopf, 1990.

Jashemski, Wilhelmina F. *The Gardens of Pompeii: Herculaneum and the Villas Destroyed by Vesuvius.* New Rochelle, N.Y.: Caratzas Brothers, 1979.

Jenkins, Ian. *Greek and Roman Life.* Cambridge, Mass.: Harvard University Press, 1986.

Jiménez, Ramon L. *Caesar against the Celts.* New York: Sarpedon, 1996.

Johnston, Mary. *Roman Life.* Glenview, Ill.: Scott, Foresman, 1957.

Josephus. *The Jewish War.* Trans. by G. A. Williamson. London: Penguin Books, 1981.

Joshel, Sandra R. *Work, Identity, and Legal Status at Rome: A Study of the Occupational Inscriptions.* Norman: University of Oklahoma Press, 1992.

Juvenal. *The Sixteen Satires.* Trans. by Peter Green. London: Penguin Books, 1974.

Kampen, Natalie. *Image and Status: Roman Working Women in Ostia.* Berlin: Gebr. Mann Verlag, 1981.

Kebric, Robert B. *Roman People* (2d ed.). Mountain View, Calif.: Mayfield, 1997.

Keppie, Lawrence. *The Making of the Roman Army: From Republic to Empire.* Totowa, N.J.: Barnes & Noble, 1984.

King, Anthony. *Roman Gaul and Germany.* Berkeley: University of California Press, 1990.

Kleiner, Diana E. E., and Susan B. Matheson, eds. *I, Claudia: Women in Ancient Rome.* New Haven, Conn.: Yale University Art Gallery, 1996.

Kollek, Teddy, and Moshe Pearlman. *Jerusalem, Sacred City of Mankind: A History of Forty Centuries.* Jerusalem: Steimatzky, 1974.

Kraus, Theodor. *Pompeii and Herculaneum: The Living Cities of the Dead.* Trans. by Robert Erich Wolf. New York: Harry N. Abrams, 1975.

Landels, J. G. *Engineering in the Ancient World.* Berkeley: University of California Press, 1978.

Laurence, Ray. *Roman Pompeii: Space and Society.* London: Routledge, 1994.

Lewis, Brenda Ralph. *Growing Up in Ancient Rome.* London: B. T. Batsford, 1980.

Liberati, Anna Maria, and Fabio Bourbon. *Ancient Rome: History of a Civilization That Ruled the World.* New York: Stewart, Tabori & Chang, 1996.

Ling, Roger. *Roman Painting.* Cambridge: Cambridge University Press, 1991.

Liversidge, Joan. *Everyday Life in the Roman Empire.* London: B. T. Batsford, 1976.

Livy. *The Early History of Rome.* Trans. by. Aubrey de Sélincourt. Baltimore: Penguin Books, 1971.

Mack, Sara. *Ovid.* New Haven, Conn.: Yale University Press, 1988.

Mau, August. *Pompeii: Its Life and Art.* Trans. by Francis W. Kelsey. New Rochelle, N.Y.: Caratzas

Brothers, 1982.

Meier, Christian. *Caesar.* Trans. by David McLintock. New York: BasicBooks, 1982.

Ovid. *Ovid's Amores.* Trans. by Guy Lee. New York: Viking Press, 1968.

The Oxford Classical Dictionary. Ed. by Simon Hornblower and Antony Spawforth. Oxford: Oxford University Press, 1996.

The Oxford History of the Classical World. Ed. by John Boardman, Jasper Griffin, and Oswyn Murray. Oxford: Oxford University Press, 1986.

Oxford Latin Dictionary. Ed. by P. G. W. Glare. Oxford: Clarendon Press, 1982.

Pascolini, Aldo. *Ostia: Return to an Ancient City.* Rome: Armando, 1979.

Payne, Robert. *The Horizon Book of Ancient Rome.* New York: American Heritage, 1966.

Pearson, John. *Arena: The Story of the Colosseum.* New York: McGraw-Hill, 1973.

Percival, John. *The Roman Villa: An Historical Introduction.* London: B. T. Batsford, 1976.

Petronius, and Seneca. [By] *Petronius: The Satyricon, and* [by] *Seneca: The Apocolocyntosis.* Trans. by J. P. Sullivan. Harmondsworth, Middlesex, England: Penguin Books, 1977.

Plinius Caecilius Secundus, C. *The Letters of the Younger Pliny.* Trans. by Betty Radice. Baltimore: Penguin Books, 1963.

Plutarch:
Life of Antony. Ed. by C. B. R. Pelling. Cambridge: Cambridge University Press, 1988.
The Lives of the Noble Grecians and Romans. Trans. by John Dryden. New York: Modern Library, 1932.

Pomeroy, Sarah B.:
Goddesses, Whores, Wives, and Slaves: Women in Classical Antiquity. New York: Schocken Books, 1975.
Women in Hellenistic Egypt: From Alexandria to Cleopatra. New York: Schocken Books, 1984.

Pompeii AD 79 (Vol. I). Boston: Museum of Fine Arts, 1978.

Potter, T. W. *Roman Britain.* London: British Museum, 1983.

Reader's Digest. *Everyday Life through the Ages.* London: Reader's Digest, 1992.

Richardson, L., Jr.:
A New Topographical Dictionary of Ancient Rome. Baltimore: Johns Hopkins University Press, 1992.
Pompeii: An Architectural History. Baltimore: Johns Hopkins University Press, 1988.

Roman Civilization: Selected Readings (Vol. 2). Ed. by Naphtali Lewis and Meyer Reinhold. New York: Columbia University Press, 1990.

Rome: Echoes of Imperial Glory (Lost Civilizations series). Alexandria, Va.: Time-Life Books, 1994.

Salway, Peter. *The Oxford Illustrated History of Roman Britain.* Oxford: Oxford University Press, 1993.

Scarre, Chris:
Chronicle of the Roman Emperors: The Reign-by-Reign Record of the Rulers of Imperial Rome. London: Thames and Hudson, 1995.
The Penguin Historical Atlas of Ancient Rome. London: Viking, 1995.

Schutz, Herbert. *The Romans in Central Europe.* New Haven, Conn.: Yale University Press, 1985.

Sear, Frank. *Roman Architecture.* Ithaca, N.Y.: Cornell University Press, 1982.

Shelton, Jo-Ann. *As the Romans Did: A Source Book in Roman Social History.* New York: Oxford University Press, 1988.

Snodgrass, Mary Ellen. *Roman Classics Notes.* Lincoln, Nebr.: Cliffs Notes, 1988.

Stambaugh, John E. *The Ancient Roman City.* Baltimore: Johns Hopkins University Press, 1988.

Suetonius. *The Twelve Caesars.* Trans. by Robert Graves. Harmondsworth, Middlesex, England: Penguin Books, 1957.

Tacitus:
The Annals of Imperial Rome. Trans. by Michael Grant. London: Penguin Books, 1989.
The Complete Works of Tacitus. Ed. by Moses Hadas, trans. by Alfred John Church and William Jackson Brodribb. New York: Modern Library, 1963.

Tingay, G. I. F., and J. Badcock. *These Were the Romans.* Chester Springs, Pa.: Dufour Editions, 1989.

Veyne, Paul, ed. *A History of Private Life: From Pagan Rome to Byzantium* (Vol. 1). Trans. by Arthur Goldhammer. Cambridge, Mass.: Belknap Press of Harvard University Press, 1992.

Vickers, Michael:
Ancient Rome. Oxford: Equinox, 1989.
The Roman World. New York: Peter Bedrick Books, 1989.

Vita Quotidiana nell'Italia Antica (Vols. 1 and 2). Bologna: COOP, Casalecchio di Reno, 1993.

Walker, Susan. *Memorials to the Roman Dead.* London: British Museum Press, 1985.

Ward-Perkins, J. B. *Roman Imperial Architecture.* London: Penguin Books, 1981.

Webster, Graham. *The Roman Imperial Army: On the First and Second Centuries A.D.* Totowa, N.J.: Barnes & Noble Books, 1992.

Wells, Colin. *The Roman Empire.* Cambridge, Mass.: Harvard University Press, 1992.

White, K. D.:
Greek and Roman Technology. London: Thames and Hudson, 1986.
Roman Farming. Ithaca, N.Y.: Cornell University Press, 1970.

Women's Life in Greece and Rome. Ed. by Mary R. Lefkowitz and Maureen B. Fant. Baltimore: Johns Hopkins University Press, 1982.

Wood, Nicholas. *The House of the Tragic Poet.* London: Nicholas Wood, 1996.

Yegül, Fikret. *Baths and Bathing in Classical Antiquity.* New York: Architectural History Foundation, 1992.

Zabern, Verlag Philipp von. *Cleopatra's Egypt: Age of the Ptolemies.* Brooklyn, N.Y.: Brooklyn Museum, 1988.

PERIODICALS

Archeo: Attualita Del Passato, July 1990.

Gentili, Gino Vinicio, and Duncan Edwards. "Roman Life in 1,600-Year-Old Color Pictures." *National Geographic,* February 1957.

OTHER SOURCES

The Fragrant Past: Perfumes of Cleopatra and Julius Caesar. Exhibit catalog. Atlanta: Emory University Museum of Art and Archaeology, April 5-June 25, 1989.

Rediscovering Pompeii. Catalog. Rome: L'Erma di Bretschneider, 1990.

INDEX

Numerals in italics indicate an illustration of the subject mentioned.

boxing, 79; *ludi*, *132-157*; plays, 149-155. *See also* Games
Epictetus (philosopher), quoted, 121
Equestrians, 22
Etruscan, Roman culture derived from, 8, 125, 141
Eumachia, Building of, 86, 87-88

F

Farmers, 59, 62, 72-75
Faun, House of the, *55*
Faustina (wife of Marcus Aurelius), 148
Festivals, 15-16, 126. *See also* Games
Fire (of AD 64), 45, 144
Fishermen, 96, *97*
Flask, oil, *80*
Florus, Gessius (governor), 115, 116
Food: banquets, 40, *41-43*, 144; markets, 82-83; and slaves, *62-63*, 64; in *thermopolia*, *83*; vendors, *96-97*
Forceps, *90*
Forum: in Pompeii, 82-83, 86; in Rome, 15-17, *16-17*
Fountains, *56, 57*
France. *See* Gaul
Freedmen, 68-71, 92, 141, 148, 154
Fulleries, 83-88, *86, 87*
Fulvia (wife of Antony), 31, 33
Funerals, *30-31, 87*, 141-142
Furnishings, 50, *51*

G

Gaiseric (Vandal king), 11
Galen (Greek physician), 142
Galilee, Judea: battle in, 116-117
Gambling, *84, 85*
Games: boxing, 79; chariot races, *132-133*, 134-141, *136-137*, *138-139*; children's, *20, 21*; dice, *84, 85*; gladiators, 141-148, *142-143, 145*; plays, 149-155; toys, *76-77*
Gardens, *48-49, 50, 57*
Gaul, 9, 99, 103, *112-113*
Germanicus (nephew of Tiberius), *110*, 111-112
Germany: mutiny in, 108-112; Roman culture in, *113*; watchtowers in, *105*
Getty (J. Paul) Museum, *57*
Girls: games, *20*, 21; protection of, 19
Gladiators, 141-148, *142-143, 145*
Gnaeus Pompeius Magnus. *See* Pompey the Great (statesman)
Gods and goddesses. *See specific names*
Golden Ass, The (Apuleius), 152-153

Governesses, 76
Gracchus, Gaius (reformer), 9
Gracchus, Tiberius (reformer), 9
Gravestone, *89*
Greece: education in, 21, 91; Philippi, 10, 30-31, 73; physicians, 90, 142; Roman culture, 8, 125, 128, 133, 151
Grocers, *96-97*

H

Hadrian (emperor), *46*, 47, 122-124
Hadrian's Wall, *122-123*, 124
Hairstyles, *22, 23*-24
Hannibal (Carthaginian general), 8
Hector (Trojan hero), 134
Helmets, *103, 138-139, 143*
Heraclas (foundling), 75-77
Herculaneum: art from, *54, 125, 130*; destruction of, 10; villas, *48-57*
Hercules (Roman god), *125*, 149, 152
Homer (poet), 134
Horace (poet), 62, 72-75
Horsemen, 106, *107*
Housing, 18 19, *48-57, 70-71*
Hypsaeus, Lucius Veranius (fullery owner), 83, 85, 86

I

Icarus (son of Daedalus), *93*, 152
Iliad (Homer), 134
Initiation ceremonies, 128, *129*
Isis (Egyptian goddess), 128, 131

J

Jerusalem, Judea: siege of, 112, 117-119; spoils from, *120-121*
Jesus, 115
Jewelry, 24, *25, 27*
Joseph ben Matthias. *See* Josephus
Josephus (Judean priest), 112, 115-120
Jotapata, Judea: siege of, 116, 119
Judea: revolt in, 112, 115-120; Roman celebration of victory over, *120-121*
Julia (daughter of Augustus), 38-39
Julia (daughter of Caesar), 22
Julia (wife of Domitian), *23*
Julia Felix (bath owner), 88
Julius Caesar. *See* Caesar, Gaius Julius
Juvenal: as poet, 146, 147; quoted, 136

K

Knifemakers, *95*

L

Lararium (shrine), 126, *127*
Late empire, *timeline* 11
Late republic, *timeline* 9-10
Latin, handwriting, *122*, 124
Latrines, public, *70*
Laundering, 83-88, *86, 87*
Law, Roman: and children, 38-39; marriage, 32-33, 38; origins, 8-9; and prostitutes, 77-78, 81; and slaves, 60-61, 64, 68, 75-77
Legionaries: construction by, *104*; foreign-born, 121; pay of, 105, 106; with standard-bearer, *110*; training, 107-108. *See also* Army, Roman
Lepidina, Sulpicia (army wife), 122, 124
Lepidus, Marcus Aemilius (governor), 10, 30-31, 33
Libertus. *See* Freedmen
Licilius (centurion), 111
Livia Drusilla (wife of Augustus), *32-33, 34*, 38, 44
Livy (historian), quoted, 8, 151
Longidienus, Publius (shipwright), *89*
Lucretia (noblewoman), 8
Ludi. *See* Games
Lupercalia festival, 15-16

M

Maecenas, Gaius (arts patron), 73, 146
Mancinus, Aulus Hostilius (official), 77-78, 81
Manilia (prostitute), 77-78, 81
Marc Antony. *See* Antony, Marc
Marcellus Theater, *map* 13, *135, 149*
March, ides of, 27-28
Marcus Aurelius (emperor), 142, 148
Marius, Gaius (consul), 9, 105, 107
Marketplaces, 82-83
Marriage: adultery, 26, 38, 77; aristocracy, 22, 32; army wives, *108-109*, 122, 124; ceremonies, 26, *27*; law, 32-33, 38
Mars (Roman god), 125
Martial (poet), 80
Masks, *150-153*
Medical profession, *90*, 142
Menu, *83*
Merchants, *94-97*
Messalina (wife of Claudius), 154
Messiah, Judean hopes for, 112, 115
Metalsmiths, 92
Metamorphoses (Ovid), 147
Military. *See* Army, Roman

Mime shows, 151-154, *155*
Minerva (Roman goddess), 86, 87
Mithras (Persian god), *131*
Mnester (actor), 154
Monarchy, *timeline* 8
Mosaics in villas, *49, 52-55, 53*
Mother-in-Law, The (Terence), 151
Murals in villas, *49-56*
Muses, *146-147*
Musicians, *42, 54, 142-143, 146, 154*
Mutinies, 108-112

N

Nero (emperor): baths of, 80; execution of Christians by, 145; and the games, 139; mother's influence on, *44*, 45; as performer, 133-134, 155-156; and slave protests, 61; statue of, *140*; suicide of, 45, 117, 156
Nerva (emperor), 45-47
Nîmes, France: and Pont du Gard, *112-113*
North Africa, and Roman culture, *115, 156-157*
Nursemaids, *74*, 75-77

O

Occupations, 89-97. *See also specific occupations*
Octavian (heir to Caesar): and Antony, 34, 105; marriages, 32-33; name change, 10, 34; reign of, 9, 10; in Second Triumvirate, 10, 30-32; supporters of, 73. *See also* Augustus
Octavia (wife of Antony), 32, 34
Odoacer (Germanic chieftain), 11
Ofellus (farmer), 62, 74-75
Oplontis, villa at, *53*
Optimates (Senate faction), 19
Ovid: as poet, 146, 147; quoted, 66, 137

P

Palmyra, Syria, theater in, *114-115*
Pantomimes, 151-154
Paris (actor), 154
Paris (mythical prince), 152-153
Patronage system, 70-71, 146-147
Pax Romana, 113
Pedanius Secundus, Lucius (prefect), 59-61
Percennius (agitator), 109, 111
Perfumes, 23, *24*
Peristyles (garden area), *50, 56, 57*
Pesuris (hirer of wet-nurse), 75-77

Time-Life Books is a division of Time Life Inc.

TIME LIFE INC.
PRESIDENT and CEO: George Artandi

TIME-LIFE BOOKS
PRESIDENT: Stephen R. Frary
PUBLISHER/MANAGING EDITOR: Neil Kagan

What Life Was Like
WHEN ROME RULED THE WORLD

EDITOR: Denise Dersin
DIRECTOR, NEW PRODUCT DEVELOPMENT:
Elizabeth D. Ward
MARKETING DIRECTORS:
Pamela R. Farrell, Joseph A. Kuna

Deputy Editor: Marion Ferguson Briggs
Art Director: Alan Pitts
Text Editor: Stephen G. Hyslop
Associate Editors / Research and Writing:
Sharon Kurtz Thompson, Jarelle S. Stein
Senior Copyeditor: Mary Beth Oelkers-Keegan
Technical Art Specialist: John Drummond
Picture Coordinator: David Herod
Editorial Assistant: Christine Higgins

Special Contributors: Anthony Allan, Charlotte Anker,
Dónal Kevin Gordon, Susan Perry (chapter text); Gaye
Brown, Catherine Hackett, Stacy W. Hoffhaus, Marilyn
Mann, Elizabeth Thompson, Myrna Traylor-Herndon,
Barry N. Wolverton (research-writing); Magdalena Anders,
Beth Levin (research); Ann Lee Bruen (research-writing,
copyediting); Susan Nedrow (index); Ann-Louise Gates
(overread).

Correspondents: Maria Vincenza Aloisi (Paris), Christine
Hinze (London), Christina Lieberman (New York).
Valuable assistance was also provided by: Angelika Lemmer
(Bonn), Ann Natanson (Rome).

Director of Finance: Christopher Hearing
Director of Book Production: Marjann Caldwell
Director of Publishing Technology: Betsi McGrath
Director of Photography and Research: John Conrad Weiser
Director of Editorial Administration: Barbara Levitt
Production Manager: Gertraude Schaefer
Quality Assurance Manager: James King
Chief Librarian: Louise D. Forstall

Consultants:
Ori Z. Soltes is the director and curator of the B'nai B'rith
Klutznick National Jewish Museum in Washington, D.C.,
and a lecturer in the National and Resident Associate Pro-
grams of the Smithsonian Institution. His lecture courses
have included "The Legacy of Ancient Greece and Rome,"
"Greek and Roman Epic," and "Daily Life in Ancient
Rome." He has also published articles and essays on a wide
range of historical topics and has written, directed, and
narrated seven documentary videos. An adjunct assistant
professor of fine arts and theology at Georgetown University and of history at the Cleveland College of Jewish
Studies, Professor Soltes received undergraduate and gradu-
ate degrees in classics from Haverford College and Princeton University.

Robert B. Kebric, a professor of Greek and Roman history
at the University of Louisville in Louisville, Kentucky, has
consulted on sections of this volume. A member of the Society for Hellenic Studies, the Society for Roman Studies,
and the Association of Ancient Historians, Dr. Kebric has
taught and written articles on many subjects, including his-
toriography, literature, art, and the ancient and modern
Olympics. He is the author of *Roman People* and three other books, and is also a published photographer.

©1997 Time Life Inc. All rights reserved. No part of
this book may be reproduced in any form or by any elec-
tronic or mechanical means, including information storage
and retrieval devices or systems, without prior written per-
mission from the publisher, except that brief passages may
be quoted for reviews.
First printing. Printed in U.S.A.
Published simultaneously in Canada.
School and library distribution by Time-Life Education,
P.O. Box 85026, Richmond, Virginia 23285-5026.

TIME LIFE is a trademark of Time Warner Inc. U.S.A.

Library of Congress Cataloging-in-Publication Data
What Life Was Like When Rome Ruled the World / by
the editors of Time-Life Books.
       p. cm.
       Includes bibliographical references and index.
       ISBN 0-7835-5452-4
       1. Rome—Civilization—Sources. 2. Rome—
History—Republic, 265-30 B.C.—Pictorial works.
3. Rome—History—Empire, 30 B.C.-284 A.D.—Pictorial
works. I. Time-Life Books.
DG78.W47 1997   97-23245
937—dc21   CIP

3 1350 00176 7815

Other Publications:
HISTORY
The American Story
Voices of the Civil War
The American Indians
Lost Civilizations
Mysteries of the Unknown
Time Frame
The Civil War
Cultural Atlas

COOKING
Weight Watchers® Smart Choice Recipe Collection
Great Taste~Low Fat
Williams-Sonoma Kitchen Library

SCIENCE/NATURE
Voyage Through the Universe

DO IT YOURSELF
The Time-Life Complete Gardener
Home Repair and Improvement
The Art of Woodworking
Fix It Yourself

TIME-LIFE KIDS
Library of First Questions and Answers
A Child's First Library of Learning
I Love Math
Nature Company Discoveries
Understanding Science & Nature

For information on and a full description of any of the
Time-Life Books series listed above,
please call 1-800-621-7026 or write:

Reader Information
Time-Life Customer Service
P.O. Box C-32068
Richmond, Virginia 23261-2068

This volume is one in a series on world history that uses
contemporary art, artifacts, and personal accounts to
create an intimate portrait of daily life in the past.

Other volumes included in the
What Life Was Like series:

On the Banks of the Nile: Egypt, 3050-30 BC
In the Age of Chivalry: Medieval Europe, AD 800-1500
At the Dawn of Democracy: Classical Athens, 525-322 BC
When Longships Sailed: Vikings, AD 800-1100